Go m

multiple streams of income.

CASHFLOW DOJO

BUILD YOUR HOME ON MULTIPLE
STREAMS OF INCOME

MARTIN SAENZ
BA, MS, MBA

SECOND PRINTING EDITION MMXX

Copyright © 2022 NIME Publishing House

Cashflow Dojo: Build Your Home on Multiple Streams of Income

DISCLAIMER

This book is meant for purely informational purposes only. Thorough due diligence is required on your part before making *any* investment decisions. Do not construe this book or any portion thereof as legal, tax, investment, or financial advice, or any other type of advice.

Nothing contained in this book constitutes a solicitation, recommendation, endorsement, or offer by NIME Publishing House, Martin Saenz, or any third-party service provider to buy or sell any securities or other financial instruments in this book or in any other jurisdiction in which such solicitation or offer would be unlawful under the securities laws of such jurisdiction.

The content in this book is general in nature and does not address the circumstances of any particular individual, investor, and/or business entity. Nothing in this book constitutes professional and/or financial advice, nor does any information in this book constitute a comprehensive or complete statement of the matters discussed or the laws relating thereto.

NIME Publishing and Martin Saenz are not fiduciaries by virtue of any person's use of or access to this book or any portion thereof.

Contents

People see you by your actions, so make your actions awesome by building your home on multiple streams of income!

This book is dedicated to Justin.
May this book honor your short life.

About the Author

M artin Saenz, BA, MS, MBA, is a professional public speaker, thought leader, real estate investment coach, best-selling author, and fund operator. Approachable, knowledgeable, and determined are all great ways to describe Martin. He is a self-made entrepreneur and successful real estate investor driven to grow asset value, income, and knowledge for his company, investors, and partners. He currently runs a twenty-five-person operation in Sarasota, Florida with his partner, Shawn Munieo, while managing around $75 million dollars in assets under management in both mortgage notes and commercial real estate.

An accomplished business owner, Martin Saenz holds a BA degree in Philosophy from UT-San Antonio, an MBA from Drexel University, and an MS in Project Management from George Washington University.

Initially, Martin and his wife Ruth managed their own successful government contracting startup company, which they later sold in 2013 to focus on their mortgage note and real estate portfolio.

Lending strategic industry insights and techniques, Martin is viewed as a mentor and accomplished industry thought leader. He regularly speaks at note and real estate investing conferences around the country, sharing extensive real estate note experience and strategies that he's built over the years.

He has written four best-selling books on Amazon, in which he gathers valuable information that's been strategically organized to teach readers how to develop and grow a real estate mortgage note investing business, whether they're new to the industry or a seasoned professional.

- In his first book, *Note Investing Made Easier*, he dives into specific methods to help almost anyone learn to start investing in the unique market for distressed mortgage notes.

- In his second book, *Secrets to Winning Government Contracts*, Martin touches on what it takes for a small business to earn prime federal government contracts.

- His third book, *Real Estate Note Investing Mentorship*, focuses on growing a successful note-investing business beyond just note buying.

- And his fourth book, *Note Investing Fundamentals*, lends key aspects for success in the note space.

Business partners Shawn Muneio and Martin Saenz are now at the helm of Bequest Funds (https://BQFunds.com/), an income fund that delivers monthly passive income to accredited investors at high yields. Its goal is to create a win-win scenario for all parties, including investors, borrowers, and fund operators. Martin runs a true passive income factory, as you will read in this book. Martin and Shawn are paving the way with their deep expertise in the real estate note investment market.

Martin Saenz's personal mission is to help families create a better life with monthly passive income while working with mortgage borrowers to attain their homeownership goals. Martin is committed to operating a win-win investment business that adds positive value to everyone's bottom line, including the communities and people he works with.

Today, for the first time ever, Martin is sharing the secrets that turned him into a cashflow entrepreneur (CFE) with several streams of income in his all-new book, *Cashflow Dojo: Build Your Home on Multiple Streams of Income*. Are you ready to join Martin Saenz and become a cashflow entrepreneur?

Utilize the following strategies, concepts, and tips to take back control of your life and set yourself on a collision course with financial independence!

CHAPTER 1

A COVID-Inspired Book

Once you understand your WHY, you'll be able to clearly articulate what makes you feel fulfilled and to better understand what drives your behavior when you're at your natural best. When you can do that, you'll have a point of reference for everything you do going forward.
—Simon Sinek

This book was inspired by COVID-19 and written during the pandemic of 2020, then later updated in 2022. In the weeks leading up to writing it, watching everything that everyone was going through, I realized that many people had no control over various aspects of their lives. These people were relying on various outlets such as the government, media, or schools to guide them in the right direction.

As a cashflow entrepreneur (CFE), this saddened me. I remember growing up in New Jersey and going charter boat fishing with friends from high school. It was a cold, rainy night, and we weren't catching a thing. Being a snot-nosed kid from Jersey, I started complaining about . . . well, just about everything. I'll never forget what the man next to me told me: if you were always going to catch something, it would be called catching. But it's not. It's call fishing because you never know. Fast-forward through nineteen years of entrepreneurship and thirteen years as a cashflow investor, and I can tell you I'm fully focused on catching versus fishing. This means I invest only in assets that will probably produce an ongoing monthly income that is consistent and predictable. Unfortunately, I see much the opposite with most investors out there today, which further inspires me to share the strategies I've learned to help people develop the ability to generate multiple streams of income for themselves.

Now, how do I define a stream of income? I would say an *income stream* is any source of income that is created to consistently produce positive cashflow into a person's account. As it relates to passive income, I would define it as any source of income that consistently produces positive cashflow into a person's account with minimal effort from the individual. Think of it like a tree that bears fruit on a regular basis. You must first plant the tree, then nurture it by giving it the right soil, nutrients, sun, and plenty of water. At some point, the tree will bear fruit consistently. The tree represents your capital investment into a passive income vehicle, and the fruit represents the positive cashflow being thrown off on a consistent basis. Most investors cut down their own trees to produce cashflow, such as selling stocks for income or saving money in case they are fired from a job. This mindset has kept many people poor for years. What I'm writing about here is growing your tree so it produces as much passive income as your active income so you can work toward living a life that is less financially stressful.

Just about anyone can survive, but I'm not talking about that. I'm talking about developing and growing multiple streams of income while maintaining what you do for active income. Furthermore, in my experience, as you grow your passive income, you become motivated to grow your active income by improving your skill set.

I want everyone to succeed, which is why I wrote this how-to book. For me and several people I know, COVID-19 has been a golden opportunity for new investments, new businesses, and new hope, but if you look out across the vast landscape of that is this country, that's not what you see. You see a lot of sad faces, a lack of control, and often even desperation.

At the same time, all the goals, the focus, the planning, and the work that occurs daily have left my family and me at a point where not that much has changed. This isn't to say that we don't feel for our community or our world where a lot of people are suffering. Rather, the healthier my family and I are, the more we can give back and help our fellow brothers and sisters—which is exactly our mission now. We measure our financial health by what we need and want to see financially against what our fruit trees are bearing.

If you're not motivated just by additional income streams and are looking for a bigger WHY, just think about all the people who need you to be at your highest point. If you're in a better position, you can help the very people who need it the most.

You probably picked up this book because you wanted more for yourself, the family you support, or the people you employ. The challenge many folks have is where to begin. I would argue that everything starts with where you are financially. Put together a financial assessment of your current situation that involves an income statement and balance statement. Measure how much passive income is earned versus active income, understanding that there is a diminishing effect to earning active income in life (i.e., everyone gets old). Based on your financial statement, how much income do you need to earn to meet your financial aspirations? Understanding these premises will help you determine your WHY and, if nothing else, will give you a cold dose of reality. The idea behind this exercise is to develop an ongoing practice of reviewing your finances over time and measuring your performance.

If you're reading this book, you understand that the world is tough, but you're ready to wake up to all the opportunities at hand and prepare yourself for any to come. However, if you're like most people, each day you wake up, go to work and deal with a jerk of a boss—or, if you are the boss, deal with everyone else.

You may even be the jerk! In any case, you make some money, come home, manage your personal life, go to bed, then wake up and repeat.

There is plenty to deal with every single day, whether you know your WHY or not. But discovering your WHY injects passion into your life and work.

This book is for those of you who know the WHY and need help advancing toward it. In *Cashflow Dojo*, we discuss the need to involve people on your journey and treat your pursuit of finding the right people as if you're on the dating scene.

Getting real with where you are financially and surrounding yourself with the right people to help you move toward your financial aspirations is the key to achieving your WHY. The law of "like attracts like" is real. The law suggests that similar things are attracted to one another. So, if you lack discipline with your money, you will surely blow it the moment you get it in your pocket. Or, if you're committed to developing and growing passive income trees, you will achieve what I consider the Holy Grail of investing.

As you move toward your goals, you will spend less time and energy on activities that bring you down. I don't know about you, but I'm growing weary of the non-stop negativity that's floating around in this world. There's so much white noise. It's so easy to succumb to that negativity, but the daily rituals we discuss in this book will ensure you get on track and stay there while chipping away at each phase of your action plan.

That's not to say I don't occasionally succumb to negativity myself. However, just to give you an example, I recently read that people were tuned into some form of media for around fifteen hours each day—and over four hours of that was spent on social media (it varied somewhat by country of origin).[1] People are spending all this time online and not really getting the value they're missing.

However, this book will help you better identify what's providing value in your life and what needs to be cut out. This is one of the first steps to getting your dojo in order. By definition, a dojo is a house of discipline, so allow me to get a little cheesy throughout the book. The daily routines and habits you currently have and how much they influence your WHY matters. I remember when my wife and I started our own business selling museum products to the federal government. For years, my daily habits were communicating with federal clients early in the morning, then driving or flying to various federal buildings for meetings, surveys, or installation projects. The nights usually ended with me drinking beer at a Buffalo Wild Wings at 10:00 p.m., drafting proposals to win new work. My WHY was to get rich and obtain material possessions. I received what I worked for and was able to purchase many commercial and residential properties as we grew our landlord portfolio, but at a serious cost. I was miserable and burned out, on the verge of a heart attack. Fast-forward to now, I spend my days educating people on the need to build more passive income to keep up with inflation and other external threats, and I feel great. Every day, I help investors earn passive monthly income that is consistent and predictable with our evergreen income fund. My daily activity mirrors my WHY.

Perhaps you're telling yourself that you don't have a fancy fund or own any cash-flowing assets beyond your nine-to-five job. I'm here to tell you I started with nothing, not even a nine-to-five job. I was fired from a corporate job in 2004 because I was horrible at playing corporate politics. My girlfriend at the time (now my wife) and I lived off credit cards and little savings to launch a business. I remember our credit card getting declined at the grocery store many times or making payroll just in time to pay bills. In fact, I vividly remember getting a client check in the mail at 11:00 a.m. when a bill was due at noon. I sat in my car, crying my eyes out in relief. So, this book is for you, wherever you are in life. Please, just stay with me here.

Rich Dad, Poor Dad author Robert Kiyosaki refers to this as the little boy inside your head who's always there, telling you that you can't do something or that you should rely on other people for your own independence. That you need to follow someone else's track in life because you're not capable of creating your own path. That you need to focus on only one job when your family needs you to have more streams of income.

In today's world, most people lower their living standards or blame others for their own shortfalls, instead of getting that second job, starting a business, doing a side hustle, or creating additional streams of income and becoming a CFE.

This book will not change your attitude or mindset, but hopefully you'll pick up some nuggets to help you move forward. I really hope that you pick today to start making major changes in your life. That you evaluate your circumstances and say, "You know what? I'm not going to accept what I'm making now. I'm not going to accept what my wife's making. I'm going to go out and do something for my family and myself that's independent of my employer's control over me."

In the end, this book is about empowerment and survival. Not that it wouldn't be nice to get additional streams of income. With the recent pandemic, it's almost mandatory. You need this for your family, to be true to them. Or, if you're involved in a church or temple, you need this to be able to give back to them. Many people depend on you, some of whom you might not even recognize. So, it's critical to develop extra streams of income.

In fact, I believe God wants you to become successful beyond your wildest expectations. Deuteronomy 8:18 states, "But remember the Lord your God, for it is he who gives you the ability to produce wealth, and so confirms his covenant, which he swore to your ancestors, as it is today." In this sense, increasing your wealth on Earth is merely stepping into the covenant that God made with his people. Now, I don't know if you're religious at all. It just gives me comfort to know that my God wants me to be successful. He wants you to succeed, as well. That way, you can be in a position to help more people.

Let's flash forward from the Old Testament to the New with a story that reiterates these truths. Mathew 25:15–30 states:

> To one he gave five bags of gold, to another two bags, and to another one bag, each according to his ability. Then he went on his journey. The man who had received five bags of gold went at once and put his money to work and gained five bags more. So also, the one with two bags of gold gained two more. But the man who had received one bag went off, dug a hole in the ground and hid his master's money.
>
> After a long time, the master of those servants returned and settled accounts with them. The man who had received five bags of gold brought the other five. "Master," he said, "you entrusted me with five bags of gold. See, I have gained five more." His master replied, "Well done, good and faithful servant! You have been faithful with a few things; I will put you in charge of many things. Come and share your master's happiness!" The man with two bags of gold also came. "Master," he said, "you entrusted me with two bags of gold; see, I have gained two more."
>
> His master replied, "Well done, good and faithful servant! You have been faithful with a few things; I will put you in charge of many things. Come and share your

master's happiness!" Then the man who had received one bag of gold came. "Master," he said, "I knew that you are a hard man, harvesting where you have not sown and gathered where you have not scattered seed. So I was afraid and went out and hid your gold in the ground. See, here is what belongs to you." His master replied, "You wicked, lazy servant! So you knew that I harvest where I have not sown and gather where I have not scattered seed? Well then, you should have put my money on deposit with the bankers, so that when I returned I would have received it back with interest. So take the bag of gold from him and give it to the one who has ten bags. For whoever has will be given more, and they will have an abundance. Whoever does not have, even what they have will be taken from them. And throw that worthless servant outside, into the darkness, where there will be weeping and gnashing of teeth."

Does that sound like a God who doesn't want you to live in abundance? It's interesting because we often get the impression that, somehow, being poor is tantamount to being a good Christian, but that's far from the truth. Regardless of what your faith is—or even if you have faith—just know that you're not only hurting yourself when you aren't increasing your WHY and stepping into the CFE lifestyle, you're hurting the people you love most.

There are four different types of adults in this country. You have (1) employees and small business owners who are financially stable, (2) employees and small business owners who are suffering financially, (3) out-of-market individuals who aren't in the workforce, whether that's with a fixed income or unemployment or whatever the case, and (4) CFEs with multiple streams of income who are moving along just fine. Our goal is to get persons 1, 2, and 3 to be more like person 4.

This would be true whether there had been a pandemic or not. But even then, what's the next big disaster going to look like? Will you be prepared? All that to say, it is more important than ever to move as many suffering people into the CFE lifestyle as possible.

This is your wake-up call!

Step 1 to becoming a CFE is to build a living financial statement for all your income, expenses, assets, and liabilities in spreadsheet format. By living, I mean a financial statement you will keep updated on a weekly basis. This is so you can meet with your accountability partner, spouse, or coach in order to review how you are performing financially. This is equivalent to joining a gym and building the weekly habits to go work out. I had my statement created by a professional I found on https://fiverr.com/ for $120 but I can email you a template if you reach out to me at martin@2cfnow.com. I have mine stored on Google Drive, so my wife and I can access it easily. For the income statement, I break things down by active income versus passive income. Active income is how you trade time for money in most cases. If you do not show up, you do not get paid. I consider passive income as income that comes to you on a monthly basis in a consistent and predictable fashion with minimal effort outside the acquisition of it. As for expenses, I have them them broken out between living expenses and business expenses which I'll delve into later in the book. For my balance statement, I use the categories of banking, passive investments, real estate, and others for assets. I look to break out assets that are directly related to the production of passive income and ones that are more associated with stores of value. For liabilities, I use current liabilities and long-term liabilities. Current liabilities are things like credit cards, and long-term liabilities can be mortgages on properties, long-term debt, and the like. I'm not a CPA or financial planner, but this system has served me well for many years. My wife is tasked with updating the financials, and we review them on a weekly basis. It's not just about the money, but sharing something very valuable with my wife so we're both on the same page. Meeting with her tends to bring up discussions about things we can do to save more money or investment strategies we need to explore. Updated statements and regular meetings also help hold you accountable to your goals.

Be honest with yourself and list everything. Meet with your family or people that you trust and review the results. Numbers don't lie and this can be a sobering experience. Then, create a separate column next to the current results and call it "future results." Here, let your creative thinking come out.

Step 2 of becoming a CFE is to visualize your WHY. So, go find a quiet place where you can spend some alone time with yourself. Close your eyes and really think about how you want to see yourself.

- How many streams of income can you see coming in?
- What asset classes or activity do you need to take part in to achieve it?
- What streams are active, and which are passive?
- How much would be enough to make you comfortable?
- How do you see yourself living with these streams of income coming in?

Focusing on your WHY will serve as your motivation to form your new disciplines and land the right passive income opportunities.

Step 3 is to do your research on additional streams of income.

Earlier in this book, I mentioned my company is a passive income factory. Let me explain what I meant. My partner and I own a private company that purchases distressed mortgages at sub-par levels. We have a full-time team that makes connections with these homeowners and helps them back on their feet with payment plans they can afford while creating a long-term cashflow for the company. This is a daily effort. Aside from this, we operate a second entity called Bequest Funds, which is a $50 million dollar 506(c) Reg D income fund that pays investors a return of 8% and 9% annually. There are no fees, and distributions are made monthly. My partner and I are the largest investors in our own fund, and we operate it every day. I talk to accredited investors daily and see if we're a fit for what they're looking to achieve. We raised large amounts of capital and deploy that capital by buying mortgages at 11–13% yields. I've been doing both business models for the past ten years and am humbled by all the passive income it has generated for me, my partners, and all our investors.

Back to you! Let's say you decide to launch a business as your means to procure additional streams of income—selling insurance, for example. Check out Facebook or LinkedIn for people or groups and start researching your community. See if you can connect with community members in person through the website Meetup.

To recap, visualization is the second step, and research is the third step. Start jotting down people and groups in your area and start immersing yourself in the industry. You don't need 100% commitment at this point, but just by taking care of these action steps, you'll start building momentum, and the execution from that will help you establish your fundamentals. This stage is the best one because you can let your mind run loose.

My wife and I sought out financial freedom when we started down our path of entrepreneurship in 2004. It wasn't until 2009 that we obtained our first real estate property, which was a building that came to house our company. We didn't have a lot of access to capital at the time, but our business was growing at a rapid pace. So, I searched Craigslist for commercial properties in my area and started calling on owners and agents. I found the perfect place for our company and asked the owner to meet up. My wife won't let me forget it, but I remember sitting in a Starbucks with the seller and telling him we would pay his full price with a 10% down payment and a seller note. He about jumped out of his chair with excitement. Needless to say, my wife wasn't too impressed with my negotiation skills at the time.

There's a gigantic power grab going on in society right now, and I think more and more people are starting to wake up to that fact, which is encouraging. There's information in abundance, but there's also a lot of white noise to sift through. You have to hustle to find good information and always be on guard for negative information. Anything that would bring you down or not contribute to your action plan needs to be pruned away. You don't need this in your cashflow dojo!

Now, when you do find good information, note the source or author. Start researching them for more information and connecting with them on social media. Find out what industry conferences they attend and other groups they're part of. If you are genuine and show yourself with humility, you'll be surprised where that will take you. Before COVID-19, my life as a CFE was watching my wife homeschool our children. Our CFE business was growing at a rapid clip whereby we were buying more and more positive cash-flowing assets. We had just signed on to purchase a building for our new headquarters. We had looked at doing a build-out for our new office. We were building a team of asset managers. Everything was moving in a very positive direction.

In terms of assets, I had my properties and mortgage notes. Now, we have dozens of income streams coming in per month, but more importantly we have an operation that produces passive income on a regular basis while serving a group of people who need help. Thus, we don't have to rely on anyone else—including the markets, which can be turbulent.

There are various types of risk inherent to traditional forms of investment that are typically broken into systematic and non-systematic forms. Then you have macro-level risks such as natural disasters or global pandemics that one simply cannot stop from happening—but one can get their house in order beforehand. You might not be able to see the future, but you can still prepare for the unknown. Your commitment to conserving what you've built and doing everything possible to push through challenging times will determine your level of success. In conclusion, step 3 is all about forming your identity as a CFE as you perform research and develop new disciplines in your life.

The fourth step of becoming a CFE is to guard your thoughts. I don't want to mislead you, though. I have doubts and fears too—we all do. But I work extra hard to push through mine.

For instance, I've had plenty of fear hit me daily since the pandemic started. I've had doubts at higher levels than normal. Throughout the day, that little boy keeps saying, "You need to back out on the office building or your headquarters or this other opportunity. You need to pull back your marketing. You need to pull back from some of these active trades." It's all a message of retreat at a level I've never seen before, and it's all based on COVID.

Now, for my part, I try not to listen to what the media, social media, or the government are putting out (on both sides of the aisle). I put my faith in God, myself, my family, and the people in my inner circle. I can't put faith in macro factors like unemployment rates, GDP, Dow Jones, or other market indices. I can't have any faith in a stock market that's more like a giant casino than anything else. At the same time, I do need to understand what the housing market looks like because it affects how I underwrite from a business standpoint. But I do try to turn down the negativity as much as possible. Another point to this is that we in society have been programmed to believe that the best course to financial freedom is through donating to Wall Street in the form of 401k's, IRA, brokerage platforms, and direct stock purchases. Changing this financial blueprint to consider multiple streams of passive income as the pathway to financial freedom is difficult for most.

Currently, I receive income from dozens of sources, as noted, and I personally vetted, created, and maintained each of these asset types. I have the most control over the performance of each of my assets. I have disciplines in place (that I didn't used to have, by the way) that took years to evolve. I'm now able to box-out the white noise, and as we start to come out of the first wave of the pandemic and businesses start to reopen, I went through with all the trades I had in the pipeline. We also bought the business space we had looked at, are finishing the build-out, are pressing forward with our marketing, and are working with a record number of new borrowers.

What areas do you feel you have the most control over? Set aside the cashflow piece for a moment. What are your areas of interest or expertise? Try googling subjects such as "making money with . . ." or "side hustle with . . ." and see what turns up. You don't need to reinvent the wheel when you can learn from people who are a few steps ahead of you. Search social media for groups that meet in your areas of interest or expertise. You can ask around about what other folks are doing to create income. Create times during the week to dedicate to this task and hold yourself accountable to doing the work, and you will be well on your way to becoming a CFE!

I view myself as a financial freedom fighter helping families create legacy wealth. I see families struggling financially and work with them daily, driven by the company's mission of "Creating a better life with one simple investment."

When society is hit with something like a global pandemic, people are hit from a psychological, physical, and financial standpoint. When that happens, you have to start concentrating on the positives, box-out the negatives, and focus on things that you can control (like the five steps of becoming a cashflow entrepreneur).

Now, ask yourself the following: Did you have goals during the pandemic? How did you survive during the pandemic? Now is not the time to scrap your goals and plans. Adjust them, but don't get rid of them altogether. Moreover, you can even use the current crisis as a means to take advantage of all-new opportunities, fine-tune systems, and extend outreach.

A whole lot of people are at home right now, too, so there's never been a better time to put the research into the people you need to connect with. People are more accessible than ever. You can call people who might normally snub you, and they will talk with you. It's a great time for outreach in this country. Again, you create additional streams of income through people, some of whom you have a relationship with and others you need to form a relationship with. During the pandemic, folks are home waiting for your call, so pick up the damn phone and get to know someone who can change your life!

Also, fill your mind with positives. Work harder than ever. Let the creative juices flow. Push everyone around you to stay positive. Come out of the pandemic better than how you came into it! Find and increase your WHY, and prepare yourself for the next major event before it happens!

Focusing on consistent income you can trust is step 5.

This step focuses on your confidence levels with the operator who is producing the cash flow and the asset itself that is producing the cash flow. The more disciplined you are with maintaining your living financial statement, uncovering your WHY and conducting ample research, the more you will align yourself with opportunities you can adequately source and vet.Some questions to consider with this step are:

- Does the opportunity provide consistent monthly income?
- How much control or trust do I have with this opportunity?
- How can I properly vet the operator?
- How much access do I have to the key players involved with the production of the cash flow?

The more familiarity you have with the opportunity, the more you can hold a confidence level with the consistency and predictability of the income being generated.

That's where the CFE lifestyle will help. And here are the five steps to help you get there:

- Step 1: Create a living financial statement
- Step 2: Visualize your WHY
- Step 3: Research additional streams of income
- Step 4: Guard your thoughts
- Step 5: Focus on consistent income you can trust

Last, I may sound as if I have it all together, but I don't want to give the impression that I don't have my own challenges. Still, I've learned a lot of lessons over the years that have made my life as a CFE better than ever. Of course, it wasn't always like this, as I had a lot of early lessons to learn. Let's discuss those lessons in the following chapters. You may be able to relate to what I went through.

CHAPTER 2

Early Lessons

Insanity is doing the same things over and over again, expecting different results.

—Unknown

Like a well-played record that's set to repeat, life is a series of cycles. The same set of songs keeps playing in the background. I memorized the words a long time ago, and sometimes I sing along for good measure. But that's also the definition of insanity.

Every so often we create all-new cycles, which I call habits. And then, when the cycle repeats, our whole reality has shifted.

The quote at the top of this chapter is often wrongly attributed to Albert Einstein. To be clear, it doesn't matter who the author is. It's just true. Our realities are a mixed bag of what we put into them—and what we let come into them. In both cases, these are things we can control if we're willing to. In other words, if you want different results, you have to think and act differently than you were before. Of course, I didn't always recognize this. I was living my own insanity. It was playing in the background like the broken record I described.

I was a young boy, growing up in New Jersey right outside the Big Apple, and I had the pleasure of learning from two very dedicated parents who loved me and my sister more than anything in the world. I often call this my do-to-myself stage versus my do-for-myself stage. During these years, I had a really bad cycle of work, earn, spend, be broke again. Compounding matters, I had what might best be described as a "bad attitude." Or maybe it's that I didn't respect authority. I didn't have many friends. I didn't apply myself when it came to school. I felt like I was being controlled or restricted which troubled me deeply.

It wasn't until later in life that I realized I was more of a control freak, which helped to isolate me from society's norms. I never fit in, no matter where I went. I was bullied and played the bully at times (I still have regrets about that).

I would work odd jobs and make money, but I never kept my money. No sooner than I had earned it, it would disappear. However, I did always have a sales edge that would come to the surface from time to time and lay the foundation that would help me later in life. At age five, I gathered some rocks in my front lawn and washed them up in a bucket with some cold water from the hose. I then proceeded to go door-to-door and sell my clean, shiny, new rocks to all the neighbors.

Later, some of the neighbors ended up telling my parents what happened, and they were none too happy. I had gone into the rock business of my own accord without consulting anyone first. And, to make a long story short, I made some money that day, but it wasn't like I realized I was conducting a business transaction at that point. I just knew it felt good. But before long, I was broke again. I needed to make more money.

Sometime later, my parents implemented a chore chart, where I would get certain amounts of money for doing certain chores, which was always very motivating. Even though I didn't excel in school, I always liked business. So, that arrangement worked well for me and taught me the value of a hard day's work and that money doesn't just fall from trees. Technically speaking, a chore chart is a merit-based system by which you can get paid. You have a bunch of activities that need to be done by someone and get paid per completed activity. So, if you're a motivated individual who wants to earn a lot of money, you can earn just about as much as you want if you put the right effort into it.

The chore chart would come roaring back to life in my household many years later when I became a father, so I appreciate learning those behaviors from my parents. I'm curious how many adults would benefit from a chore chart of sorts. They teach the discipline of scheduling, creating predictability, and working on multiple streams of income.

Being a CFE is more about creating activities that generate more active and passive income in your life than it is about being a full-blown entrepreneur. This could mean your plan is simply to develop a side hustle, get a second job, or invest in assets. Regardless of your direction, it's important to move with the current and follow the five steps:

- Step 1: Create a living financial statement
- Step 2: Visualize your WHY
- Step 3: Research additional streams of income
- Step 4: Guard your thoughts
- Step 5: Focusing on consistent income you can trust

I want to mention something important related to step 1. Perhaps this is you or not, but many folks in the US have an issue with managing their finances. This is mostly due to not forming the habit of creating an accurate financial statement and regularly reviewing it with a partner. When you do this, you start thinking creatively about ways you want to earn additional income. You will also get a bird's eye view of places you need to stop spending money. This is the foundation for your dojo and needs to be a ritual more than a practice.

When you go through the rest of the steps, just remember that the income may come in through either active or passive means. The other day, one of my employees came into my office and asked me how she can manage her money better. When I walked her through step 1, she told me she couldn't do it and asked for some books to read or practices to put in place. I told her what I'm saying to everyone reading this book: "I can't help you if you're not willing to transform and start rebuilding your financial foundation." Ironically, this person still works for me and helps me further build my financial foundation.

I follow similar steps when I'm speaking to high-net-worth individuals each day. I start with what I call "Doing the math." I always ask the investor how much income they need to maintain their standard of living. The answer is usually between $20K and $40K, but let's go with $20K for simple math purposes. I then ask them how much monthly passive income they have coming in consistently. Well over 50% of the time, the answer is zero or close to it. They typically proceed to tell me their money is tied up in the stock market, some real estate properties, bonds, 401k, and the list goes on. I then ask how long they have until they wish to retire. Let's say the answer is ten years. Well then, we have to build $20K of monthly passive income over the course of the next ten years. The math looks as follows:

- Investor needs to get from $0 in monthly passive income to $20K in ten years.
- With the Bequest Income Fund paying out at 9% annually, you can invest $2,700,000 over the next ten years and you will achieve $20K in monthly passive income.

The point of this exercise is to help the investor see things from a very different perspective. These investors tend to be highly intelligent and have been successful in their areas of expertise. But somewhere along the way, many of them bought into a flawed model that tells folks to earn, buy stocks and bonds for appreciation, and cash out when they get older. It's a model Wall Street, the government, financial media, and the school system all promote. The problem is it's a model of hope—hope that the appreciation occurs while you have zero control over the process. This is why one of my principals is to only invest in assets I control. Ironically, "control" is used loosely. I do invest in other cash-flowing funds, but I know the operators and have proximity to their operation.

In my earlier days, the problem was my work-earn-spend-be-broke-again model, and if I had a goal or better understood my financial predicament, I could have channeled my energy a little bit better. And my money could have been more productive too. Having goals would also have made me more disciplined, something needed to succeed in life.

I had no plan. I had no action steps (more on this topic soon). I didn't have the sense to do any of that, so I was just going through life carefree and reckless.

My mother was a teacher for most of her life, and my father worked at Bell Labs Research as a computer scientist. Both were intellectual individuals, but neither of them thought in terms of business. Entrepreneurship or small business ownership would have been foreign words to them back then. Now, that's not to say that they weren't excellent providers. They spent a great deal of time working so my sister and I had a good childhood. So, that was their focus—their action plan.

Meanwhile, at an early age, I was learning all this stuff that would pay out in big ways as I got older. I was still stuck in the work-earn-spend-be-broke-again model for a while longer, but I was trending in the right direction and learning the tricks and tips of business that would pay out for me later.

In conclusion, it's important to build a merit-based reward system in your life so you can gain control over your income. But before any of this can happen, you must get your financial house in order. What's your dojo looking like?

CHAPTER 3

An Unexpected Blessing

> *The only thing that's keeping you from getting what you want is the story you keep telling yourself.*
>
> **—Tony Robbins**

There's a similar quote by Jim Rohn that I also like. He said, "The only way it gets better for you is when you get better. Better is not something you wish, it's something you become." He's saying it doesn't happen overnight. It's something you have to consciously work at, similar to the five steps of becoming a CFE in the first chapter.

In 1992, I was living in North Jersey driving a souped-up Trans Am, jamming out to some of my favorite freestyle music, working several small jobs in restaurants, and going clubbing on the weekends. Hey, life was pretty good. I lived rent-free at my parent's house. I had the freedom to come and go as I pleased. I no longer had the restrictions of school. I was in a very free state, and it was clear I wasn't going to attend a four-year school at that time.

So, I decided to enroll at Union County Community College, which was about fifteen minutes from my house. One of the first classes I took was English, and my teacher was a short, balding African American gentleman. (By the way, if that teacher—or anyone—had told me I would end up writing multiple books, I would have laughed. But that's a whole other issue.) This professor was a nice man, and he wore a top hat. He was very soft-spoken and unique in his mannerisms. He really seemed to be at peace with himself. On the first day, he introduced himself to everyone. Shortly thereafter, he handed us a book by Richard Wright called *Black Boy* and told us to write an essay about it after we were done.

Now, what struck me as odd was that the class structure was very rigid throughout my K–12 days. But now, here was this nonchalant man who didn't seem to care if we did the homework or not. He may as well have said, "If you want to excel here, this is the expectation, but I'm not going to lose any sleep if you don't take it seriously."

I have to admit, I liked that. His whole demeanor was unlike anything I'd ever witnessed in a classroom. Needless to say, I picked up the book and started reading it immediately, and I'm glad I did.

I found myself totally immersed in the whole story of *Black Boy*. I also later read *Native Son*, and I was struck by Wright's tone and style. They were wonderful stories, and I became captivated by classroom learning for the first time in my life. Writing the essay was freeing because it no longer felt like a chore. I mean, I actually wanted to write it! That was the type of educational structure I thrived in. Had K–12 been based on that same format, I feel like I would have done much better, but it was too rigid for my tastes.

Since then, I've encountered numerous other people who expressed they had gone to or were going to go to community college too. When they tell me this, they often hang their heads in shame as if they've done something wrong. Or they feel like they haven't accomplished their full potential because they haven't gone to a four-year college.

To those individuals, I'd like to say that community college changed my life! I'm thoroughly convinced, had I gone to a traditional four-year college right out of high school, I would have never made it. I would have dropped out so fast that I would have ended up back at my parent's house in shame.

I just didn't have the discipline to succeed at the four-year level right away. And community college allowed me to ease into the whole college situation and acclimate to the demands of higher education. It was challenging to some degree, but it wasn't full-on immersion either, where you're living on campus, getting involved in the social scene, and totally engrossed in the whole atmosphere. Community college prepared me mentally to succeed at the next level.

I can now report that I went on to graduate with a bachelor's degree in Philosophy from a four-year school. I worked a few low-end jobs along the way, but had I not taken those first few steps the way I did, nothing would have happened for me.

I also learned this world is tough and cruel when you get a liberal arts degree! But after a lot of struggle, I did manage to get a job. I started working as a mortgage officer in a large company with over seven hundred other mortgage officers.

With time, I was able to work my way up and become the second-highest-producing mortgage officer in the company. As for the person who was number one, in hindsight, I've often thought there were some shenanigans or foul play involved. But I won't harp on that for too long. This training in sales laid the foundation for every business deal I've been involved with ever since.

I learned the following:

1. Planning out my day the afternoon before helped me succeed and not be distracted throughout the day.

2. Control over my earnings was a powerful force that motivated me to do more than I normally would have done.

3. The more I sold, the more people I could help—from both a personal and professional standpoint.

Around that time, I married my high-school sweetheart too. But I learned after that when you marry a high school sweetheart there's a significantly higher probability for divorce, and I definitely added to that statistic. We went through a bitter separation, but I'm proud to say that things worked out in the end for everyone.

After the divorce, I started charting my own path and became more independent, not just relationship-wise, but including all the external factors that seek to infiltrate your circumstances and control your life.

However, I still didn't have a rock-solid plan.

If you don't have a plan, you're working on someone else's plan. So, it's up to you to decide which one you want to do. Please choose wisely.

While you are spending some time planning your steps to building multiple streams of income, it's important to reflect on your journey along the way. What were some of your pain points and how did you grow from them? Are you at a pain point now and need to reach the growth phase? How does it look for you? Asking yourself some tough questions will help your planning process so as you formulate ideas you can find ways to avoid potential pitfalls. Also, you can reflect on your strengths and weaknesses. As an exercise, go ahead and jot down five strengths and five weaknesses you have.

Strengths:

1)
2)
3)

4)

5)

Weaknesses:

1)

2)

3)

4)

5)

How can your money-making ideas and research play into your strengths?

One of the strengths I developed was a passion for higher education. I went on to enroll in an MBA program at Drexel University and relocated to Philadelphia. The understanding was that your average MBA earns just north of $106,000 per year (per *US News and World Report*). So, I felt like that was something I needed to do. Looking back, it's interesting how so many people believe a more expensive education will solve their money problems. It's probably because that is an outdated concept still driven by our country's institutions.

I don't remember many of the theories that I learned in business school, but I remember a discussion I had with my sister's boyfriend, Peter, during my graduation party. Peter was a successful business owner and real estate investor with just a high school degree. He grabbed his pockets and told me that is where he holds his MBA. I wanted that MBA too.

"I need to increase my income," I thought. "Then everything will be fine." If you recall chapter 1, the basic model is the same, but earning more money helps nonetheless.

At the end of the day, I did receive a job as a unit manager at a call center—but I never factored in all the expenses. As you increase your income, the number of variable expenditures increases as well. You're probably paying a mortgage, taxes go up, and living expenses don't have to increase but tend to do so.

To make a long story short, I was left with no disposable income even though my earnings had gone up considerably. A few years before, I was working for a third of the pay and had no disposable income. Now, I was earning more but still had no disposable income.

I had taken all these steps but was at the same point, which was utterly baffling. In fact, I was probably at a worse point because I now had student loan debt to boot. I couldn't help but think, "What's the point?"

If you have any chance of success, you must develop financial discipline in your life. With that said, not to the point of making the buffalo cry as you pinch a nickel. You need to have a sense of how much money comes in and how much goes out.

Building additional streams will initially require money to go out, but that can be limited with more sweat and hustle. So how do you bootstrap the process? The answer is simple: committed research to determine the right areas to focus on and who the key relationships need to be with. Then, you build what I call an outreach matrix to hold yourself accountable and help you build daily rituals that move you closer to your goals. The matrix looks something like this:

	Monday		Tuesday	
Activity:	Goal:	Actual:	Goal:	Actual:
Research	90 min.	40 min.	90 min.	30 min.
Events attended	60 min.	0 min.	60 min.	60 min.
Social Media connections	40 min.	50 min.	40 min.	40 min.
Phone calls	60 min.	35 min.	60 min.	50 min.

As I'm writing this book, I am preparing to present a concept to Grant Cardone—whom I interviewed in June 2020 —for consideration. This relationship is still in its infancy, but it has cost me no money to date. Just good, old-fashioned outreach and the cost of cell phone service.

What's interesting is that if you read any books by Gary Vaynerchuk, Grant Cardone, or Robert Kiyosaki—all these great thought leaders in real estate investing, entrepreneurship, and thought leadership—they will all tell you that college isn't for everyone. Some people are better off not taking that step and going the traditional route. They spend the time and money you would spend on college and spend it on building a business instead, which may be a better path for some people (and to be fair, at least it's a path).

Had I started entrepreneurship at an earlier age, for example, I'd probably be much further ahead today than I am. I don't look back much, but if I did, that's probably what I would have to admit.

I also realized that working that job after going to school, while working on the MBA, was relying on a single stream of income, which is very dangerous. You should shore up your sole source of income before exploring additional streams; however, you should not do this to the point of exhausting all your resources and energy. Additional streams of income require effort as well. In other words, there must be a balance.

What I have found is that when I develop additional streams of income, they are interconnected with my initial source of income. They end up playing off and strengthening each other. For example, when I sell a book, it helps me sell an online course, which, in turn, helps me connect with other like-minded folks working toward financial freedom—some of whom partner with me on the income fund, and others read more of my books.

What most couples and families are doing—at least in the US market—is having both parties work. It's easier to feel more secure when there are two incomes, so that certainly makes sense. But you'll find, later in this book, that you shouldn't really rest until you have dozens of streams of income pouring in. That is, even once you get a couple, you shouldn't rest. You should keep building cashflow as things progress. This creates velocity with your money. Also, if you pour active income into passive investments, you'll find yourself pushing to increase your active income as it becomes an inner challenge. It is like a law of nature, perhaps. Another point to make is that as you stretch yourself with income, you will elevate your goals and be of greater service to this world.

Most people think they can get to five or ten sources of income per month and then go rest on a beach somewhere drinking margaritas with the little umbrellas in their drinks all day. That's simply not true. There should be an ongoing effort to keep building cashflow streams and monitoring the cashflows. Just like in step 1, where you build and actively monitor your financial statement.

In 2001, I was hired by Sears Roebuck to manage a 120-person credit call center. I got to see first-hand the significance behind the financing department and the role those accounts played in the company's bottom line. I was also able to watch how customers consumed credit cards. There's a lot of money to be made in finance charges.

Customer loyalty was built around the department store credit card model. If you get someone using one of those cards—and paying the subsequent fees and rates—they're far more likely to continue shopping with you for months and even years into the future.

That's how Sears (and many other major brick-and-mortar retailers) was built as a company.

If you want to buy something, for example, you're going to go to the store where you have a credit card; at least, that's the thinking, and it used to be true. It still is for many people.

My unit was the call center, and not only did we help people with their issues, but we were a sales arm of the company. We would continuously encourage people to open new lines of credit, for example, by giving them offers and promotions.

Sears had a traditional corporate structure, which was based on hierarchy and seniority. During that time, I learned a valuable lesson that carried on throughout life, which was that I was very much in charge of running contests and driving motivation to make sales happen. I did several different sales promotions but the one thing I noticed that worked the best—and motivated people the most—was incorporating scratch-off tickets into the rewards system. To some people, it probably served as an additional stream of income, but that worked for us, corporately speaking.

Here's how sales promotions drive additional streams of income:

1. They allow you to take ownership of the process. My asset managers fielded calls at night and weekends, as they would get paid when the phone rang. If they

weren't compensated with promotions and bonuses, I suspect the call would have gone to voicemail more often than not.

2. They signal to your team what the level of priority is. You typically promote what is important for your business and its survival. What better way to reinforce what is important than to pay someone to own it?

3. They're fun, and it breaks up the monotony of the day-to-day workload, whereby expectations have been set in stone.

The point is that you can be creative in terms of who is doing the actual work for the additional income stream. "It's not all about you, Marty," as my sister liked to tell me growing up.

Over a few years, I had grown complacent (or stuck in the corporate rut, if you will). So, it allowed my wife and I to think about everything. I was miserable working in corporate America. It was like going to a death sentence. I felt like I had so much more to give.

I knew there was something in me that was meant to live a life of entrepreneurship. I just knew it deep down, even though I had fought if for so many years by taking the easier corporate route. I say "easier" because even though the hours can be long and hard, at the end of the day you're following someone else's plan. Having read all these books from Stephen Covey, Robert Kiyosaki, Grant Cardone, Tony Robbins, Dale Carnegie, et al., and knowing I had something brewing inside me that had not been given ample time to thrive, I was forced into making an all-new plan.

How can building additional streams of income free you from your current situation? What would you do differently if you had this security? What about your life brought you to read this book? How does it play into your WHY? Actually, the better question is, what actions are you going to take from this point forward to achieve additional income?

Sometimes, in life, we have these moments where we can slow down, take a step back, and glimpse the bigger picture. Some people call it a "moment of clarity," but it's when you finally wake up from a fog that has you going through the motions like a mindless zombie. It starts with thinking about your heart. What do you really desire?

That's where you know you need to be. Chances are, it's not where you're at, so you know you need to be someplace else.

Yet, even when you grow your income levels above your expenses and start feeling comfortable, you're still playing someone else's game. The challenge is to learn the rules and use them to your advantage. It is best to realize this and get fed up. Realize you deserve better for yourself financially, even if you love what you do. I probably read every book I could find that was motivational or business-related. I must say, Robert Kiyosaki's book, *Rich Dad, Poor Dad*, became our bible, which is probably why I quote it so often. For over twenty years, my wife and I have consumed a lot of his content and traveled around the country to participate in various investment workshops and seminars as well.

We absorbed as much information as we could. We also got inspiration from educating ourselves. It's like my old English professor who changed my life. The cycle was coming back around. We were reading everything we could and becoming more and more inspired by the day. We wanted to have something that would serve as a foundation, something we could commit to, something that we could grow from scratch, where we could produce income on our own terms, not someone else's.

Now, some people go into real estate for transactional purposes, whether as a broker, bird dogger, private money lender, or something else. Not to take anything away from them, but we wanted to have positive cashflow that we could leverage into other streams of income later. In other words, we weren't simply trying to produce transactional income, or income where you perform a service or provide a product in exchange for a fee. The goal was to build streams that were repeatable and built off each other, such as landlording, long-term money lending, insurance sales, landscaping services, and the like.

Here are some rules of thumb I've learned along the way:

1. At some point, you must bet on yourself financially. Learn as much as you can before you put your money out and you will have more confidence when you do.

2. The energy flow for your efforts must feel organic. If it doesn't, something is off, and you need to figure out what it is. "Know thyself," as Socrates put it.
3. Never stop learning.
4. Create income chain links for yourself. Each month, I have passive income hitting my account and I turn around and reinvest into another asset that produces income or a long-term store of value. I do this daily now, which is referred to as daily dollar cost averaging.
5. Always strive for greater velocity once you're up and running. If you have a flow working from the repeated sale of a product on eBay, how can you sell ten more like it?
6. As Jim Rohn put it, "always be pruning your bushes or the weeds will come." Cutting out negativity and white noise is a constant activity you must uphold.

Early on, we wanted to prove—as much to ourselves as anyone else—that we could put systems in place that would yield the kind of consistent results we needed to see. Plus, we were in government contracting, so consistency and having the right processes were really key. CFEs are interested in creating recurring flows of income through repeated or various orders from existing clients.

For example, with government contracting, our company still holds a blanket purchase agreement with the Pentagon to provide museum exhibit services. It's a contract for $4 million annually, one the company still holds even after my wife and I sold it. The government can simply request a project from our company within this blanket agreement and the order will count against the dollars set aside for the contract. Many corporations have these same types of contracts in place. So, be thinking about how you can negotiate long-term plays with people that are putting money into your pocket.

If you don't have these ingredients, you won't be sustainable. I'll elaborate. You need cashflow that pays for living expenses and investment capital. For us, initially, that was small business ownership, then landlording, and now operating several mortgage note and commercial real estate funds. I attribute what we now manage to God and living by my rules of thumb.

What we found out over time is to focus purely on what we were passionate about. I know so many people say to focus on what you're passionate about and money will come later, but I believe you should focus on what's going to be profitable and what you can build a skillset for. If you're profitable, you'll develop a passion for it. I'm sure after you reflect on your WHY and determine what drives you, there are "acres of diamonds" awaiting you.

We decided we would sell to the largest buyer in the entire world (the federal government). We were in the so-called beltway at the time, and we started a government contracting company in 2005 to further gain control of our time and income. If we were going to grow a business with multiple streams of income, we figured to go after the largest fish. That was our next big move. Step 1 involved our mindset and knowing we had to make a change and put a plan in place. Then things would get more tangible.

We opened the business out of the basement of our home with the mission to only sell directly to the federal government on a prime level—which was a bold move because many small businesses in the DC area and around the world that sell to the federal government normally sell through companies (i.e., the big boys) that hold prime contracts through the government. They get the crappiest assignments. They get paid late. They get pushed on deadlines and everything else. In short, they get the crumbs.

But we didn't want to be a part of that. We knew it would take us more time and capital (which we didn't have much of), but we were going to sell directly to the feds. So, we took out a bunch of high-interest credit cards to the tune of $225,000 to start our company. We bought equipment, paid payroll, paid the debt with debt, and went all in. It was either going to make us or break us, but we were already broke, so the risk didn't seem that big for us.

We joined the Chamber of Commerce as well as a networking group (BNI) and hit the ground running with very little money in the bank. We just had heart and commitment. Sometimes the community you build around yourself can control your stream of income. In our case, we became involved in networking groups with other small businesses that stunted our growth, instead of spending this same effort with government contracting groups that would lead to more prime federal work.

If you want to know true love, try starting a business when you're broke and hungry. If your partner stays with you from the beginning (with no other sources of income except for what you're trying to do), you have a keeper.

We could have focused on the low-hanging fruit. It was a museum exhibit company, so we sold displays and high-end signage that went in government buildings, corporate offices, art-related, and the like. We could have sold banners to every mom-and-pop shop in town, but we knew those individuals would want the lowest price or have trouble paying, so we didn't want to focus on that.

We decided to hold onto our energy and resources while we learned how to master selling to the federal government and the art of producing the product, which is its own undertaking. The idea was to gain momentum and build our foundation as we proceeded.

At this point, though we were buried in debt and had a fraction of the resources the big boys had, we felt invincible. We didn't really understand the federal market at first. We didn't even understand our craft or the competitive landscape. I guess the swagger just came from the freeing feeling of being independent and in creation mode. All in all, as you commit to step 3 of researching additional streams of income, it ramps you up the learning curve.

We were going to learn as we went along, which most people would find nerve-racking. But it was further building out our plan, so we were happy (despite the debt).

However, at the time, we didn't realize we had no rock-solid goals in place. We had a general plan in the sense we were charting our own course—but we didn't have a formal action plan. Looking back, that's one of the things I would have done differently. With that said, I recommend not leaving any money on the table with your current position or business (e.g., can you moonlight in sales for your company, can you sell more services to an existing client). At all my companies, I implement the Golden Rule. As an employee, you don't have to come to me to ask how you can make extra money. There is a clear rule in place: if you bring us a client or investor you will receive a referral fee.

I wish we'd had something more formal to guide us—and that's at the heart of why I'm writing this book.

Note: I want to provide anyone looking to build out additional streams of cashflow with a road map to follow. I'm telling you all this because you can't go haphazardly through your next five or ten years.

We are going to cover the process by which you can take your goals to fruition. However, to get the most from this book, you will want to do the following:

1. Fully understand your financial situation.

2. Determine how you can go earn more with your current income stream.

3. Figure out what industries or areas of expertise you have that might have that can yield streams of income.

4. Write down all the people in your network of influence.

Figuring all this out will require self-reflection and research, so get to work sooner rather than later. You'll grow a lot faster if you plot your course and have a much better learning curve along the way if you prepare. It's as the adage goes: "A smart man learns from his own mistakes, whereas a wise man learns from the mistakes of others."

Rest assured, it is a choice.

You have a plan, whether it's yours or someone else's, so you may as well make it your own and do something with it.

My wife and I didn't have that structure way back then. When you have that formal plan and you're living it through the rituals you put in place, you'll become consumed by the elements of the plan. You'll think about it as you're driving or taking a shower, or having supper with family. I hate to admit it, but it's true. Hopefully, my wife will gloss over that last part, but I cannot leave it out. Your plan will be all-consuming.

The fact is, it's hard to shut off once it's on. I love my family more than any business plan I can fathom, but it's my obligation and purpose in life to take care of them. So, there's no shutting it off.

A plan is much different from something you jot down on a piece of paper and forget. It's something you live and breathe. When you're using your creative juices, it's exhilarating and freeing.

God—or whatever higher power you believe in—gave us our creative abilities. The more you use them, the more freedom you have, and the more you're able to produce and make society a better place for all of us. I assume you're reading this book because you need help figuring out a plan and which actions to take to get you closer to your goals. That's what I'm striving for, and I hope this book helps you to strive a little closer to that as well. You will need this phase in your overall plan to obtain truly great freedom and sustainability.

As we grew our company into a multi-million-dollar operation, we bought a building and moved the company from our house in 2009. Before that, we paid off all the bad (high-interest) debt and bought our equipment outright. We were officially solvent, but it took about three or four years of struggle to get to that point.

Although it happened over the course of several years, going from being buried in debt to being solvent felt like flipping a light switch. My life changed for the better as I started to see the fruits of all our hard work and planning.

You may feel like a frog in a frying pan. You're okay in the pan until the heat gets turned up and you start to cook.

We weren't going to rely on Wall Street or a 401k in some corporate job. We're not mutual fund people, so if you're looking for market advice, you may be in the wrong place.

Instead, let's talk more about the business that's made more people millionaires than any other in the world: real estate.

Everything I had done was to start building an empire in real estate, and we saw a lot of people working tirelessly for years. Companies are using people up and burning them out every day. The business controls you, and the thing you go into business for—freedom—turns into enslavement.

Now, I'm a business owner at heart, but I also knew that the mistakes I was seeing in others weren't going to be for my wife and me. We were going to actually own the building we operated out of. Quickly thereafter, we bought the space next to us and started renting it out too. We had our first tenant paying us rent—which was an additional stream of income.

I must admit, I had a little too much swagger after that. I had one tenant and felt like a real estate mogul—a la Sam Zell—overnight, though that was far from the truth.

However, your mindset can take you a long way.

We rolled all our profits into additional investments, which is when things start moving much faster. We bought commercial and residential properties in the DC area. We still hold and manage those properties today. Now, some of them are on fifteen-year notes and only have about six years left as I'm writing this book. At that point, we'll probably maintain the renters for cashflow or sell the property with seller financing. Either way streams of income will be continued.

At the time I'm writing this, we are purchasing a new commercial space for our headquarters in the Fredericksburg area, so I'm still actively involved in real estate, aside from what we'll be discussing later in this book.

As it relates to creating a plan for yourself, keep the following things in mind:

1. Take full ownership of everything that happens to you in your life,

2. Think big, plan big,

3. Draft a formal written plan. I knew that I would never be taken care of by anyone but myself, so I had to focus on building long-term flows of income for my later years. Plus, there's something tangible about physical assets you can touch.

Positive cashflow is the ultimate sexiness. Interacting with tenants who pay you on time is something we all strive for—and not just from a monetary perspective. You're providing people a home or a building to operate their business out of. Two of my properties are actually occupied by churches, so there's a spiritual angle. I'm able to help promote the worship of God. So, you can see how investing in real estate actually has numerous facets to it.

I realized later that I was growing, but I was still thinking small. I didn't have a formal plan in place. I didn't have a visualization of where I wanted to be or needed to go. I had limited streams of income based on single-occupant tenants. Fortunately, the DC area has been relatively recession-proof because the federal government keeps growing, so I have no vacancies in either my residential or commercial properties. The irony is, buying single-occupied real estate is like having one stream of income from one source. Thus, if they move out, 100% of your income stream from that source dries up and leaves you vulnerable. This is something to keep in mind as you research the income streams you will be generating.

I've had close to zero vacancies, which is practically a miracle, and I realize that's not as likely to happen in certain pockets of the country. So, you have to really understand your market. Look at what's going on today, with the COVID-19 pandemic. There are all these Airbnb property owners who can't rent out their properties because people can't travel. So, they cannot pay their mortgages or other expenses. That's a reflection on buying into a single-occupancy opportunity.

Wherever you are, look at the people who've been in the same space for about ten or twenty years—like I did with other museum exhibit companies that sold to the government. I knew my competitors. Some of them had been in business for over fifty years. They had 100,000-square-foot facilities. They had 80–100 (or more) employees. They were well known in the space. They owned their own business spaces. They were solvent. As business owners, they were very affluent.

That was my competition, but that's how you can see your future. You're not necessarily going to become them, but it may give you an idea of what your future might look like if you keep playing by their rules. So, you always want to do a deep dive into the competition. Know what's going on in your area, your niche, your market, your ideal customers, et cetera

What if you're looking for something different from that? You can use your competition's example as a baseline to craft your own plan. What are the attributes you like about these players who are established within your business model? What is it that you don't like?

We'll be elaborating on some of these ideas and how to take action with your plan later in this book.

CHAPTER 4

Setting Standards

Shoot for the moon, because even if you miss, you'll land among the stars.

—Les Brown

L et's think about what elements control most people. I'd have to say low standards are at the forefront. You may work hard enough to get by. If so, you're not alone. That's what a lot of people do. They work just hard enough to meet their minimum obligations, and no more. Not to mention, as a society we aren't getting challenged. Think about school, work, media, and the like. They don't challenge our minds. Yes, there's plenty of white noise (by way of cute cat videos on YouTube or funny memes on Facebook, for example), but nothing that pushes us to be our best.

There are no high-quality standards either, unless you count the traditional life model.

From an early age, we're told to go to college, get married, and buy a home, which constitutes what I'd simply call the traditional model. There's nothing inherently wrong with any of these elements. However, we haven't done a good job in this country of teaching the value of financial literacy, entrepreneurship, and creativity—three of the essential ingredients of the CFE lifestyle.

Society is really rigid. It's good at churning out good citizens or employees who give their money to banks and Wall Street and don't disrupt the traditional model. Going outside this track used to leave many people on the outs. However, there's a growing acceptance of alternative paths. The best way to start setting new standards for yourself is to take control of your self-education (i.e., what you feed your mind).

Recall the five steps:

- Step 1: Create a living financial statement
- Step 2: Visualize your WHY
- Step 3: Research additional streams of income
- Step 4: Guard your thoughts
- Step 5: Focusing on consistent income you can trust

By now, I hope you've built your financial statement and have determined your WHY. This is the point where you focus on the third step, which is researching options for additional streams of income. There are people like Gary Vaynerchuk, who said, "If you live, breathe and sleep entrepreneurship, and you have shown some ability and talent before the age of eighteen, you should really consider your opportunities and whether or not it makes sense to go to college. "

Robert Kiyosaki is another proponent of alternative paths. He said, "We go to school to learn to work hard for money. I write books and create products that teach people how to make their money work hard for them."

There are several resources nowadays that can give people training, education, and confidence in a range of areas. There are whole courses you can take for a fraction of the cost of college. If you go to places like Udemy, for instance, courses are $200 or less. Use your time wisely. You may want to start by searching https://udemy.com/, where they have over a hundred thousand online courses in just about every subject you can think of. Chances are, there's a course that you're a subject matter expert in that someone is earning income on today.

There are many other resources out there—too many to list—but you get the idea. Simply put, if you want to learn about insurance, real estate, investing, graphic design, video production, computer programming, or anything else you can think of, there are more opportunities beyond the traditional model than ever. So, I would encourage you to check those out, do your due diligence, and consider the online route to further your skillset.

Most research will not cost you a penny but is priceless in its value. You can join a Facebook or LinkedIn group on any subject matter. Experts, passionate souls, and novices tend to occupy these groups and share content with everyone. That said, there are also bad groups that share bad content and bad players that share useless information. Therefore, it's good to engage with several groups and have a litmus test for filtering out information that does not lead you to your goals. This, of course, is step 4.

College is not for everyone. If you have the determination and self-discipline to be self-taught, you might try an alternative path such as the one I pointed out. You could come out at a significant advantage over others around you—unlike the forty million student loan borrowers.

I'm not saying you shouldn't go to college, just that it's important to evaluate all the options. There may be a better path forward depending on your individual goals or expectations as well as your level of discipline.

My goal is to get you out of thinking single-mindedly and racking up $100,000 or more in student loan debt, often for a degree you can't use. Plus, you'd be amazed at the useless information you have to absorb along your college track while learning the lessons you need to advance. I have a bachelor's and two master's degrees, so I'm speaking from experience.

Whatever plan you have, whether it entails growing your active income or your passive income, it needs to involve human interaction. You can find the right in-person groups to connect with like-minded individuals at https://meetup.com/, Facebook, LinkedIn, Chamber of Commerce, and more. Before you attend meetings, make sure you have a game plan. Here are some steps you can take:

1. Research participants that attend or are in the group.
2. Connect with them on LinkedIn and other social media platforms.
3. Have a goal for your participation, such as finding a mentor or meeting two people that earn income from the area of interest.
4. Dress sharp.
5. Be humble and genuine. Fake it until you make it is a bad look for anyone.
6. Evaluate the results after the meeting.

The old-school model of thinking was that once you pay off your home, you're free from the responsibility of making payments. However, what more people are understanding is that your home is a liability, not an asset. You're tied to insurance, upkeep and taxes, so in the end there's nothing free about that at all. Also, this can distract your focus on buying real estate properties for cashflow purposes.

People are being controlled by society's track (as mentioned above). This relates to education, buying a home, and investing in the stock market. With society's pull, they almost make you feel like you're inadequate if you don't live according to their plan.

When I finished high school, I graduated with barely a C average. The school I went to had a very high rate of students going to college afterward and a low drop-out rate. However, to achieve those numbers, they put people who were underperforming—such as myself—into a trailer next to the high school for a program called Project 79, which was a dumbed-down version of a school where they lowered the standards just to keep their statistics (and any funding tied to those statistics) high. Teaching people like me—who learn through visualization and activity versus memorization and regurgitation—is not an option in public schools.

School systems and the government want you to conform because it feeds their agenda.

Remember how I said there's always control, whether you have it or not? Well, that's what I was referring to! At the end of the day, someone is always going to be in control of your situation. So, who's it going to be? That's a question that you can answer for yourself. Is the government or traditional education system going to control you? Or are you going to control yourself and embark on the CFE lifestyle? Hence, it's critical to realize that no institution can help you become a CFE, but the right people can.

The employer will always control the employee just by virtue of giving them a stream of income. It's not so much their rules, the employee handbook, or your rigid schedule. They control you by only opening up one stream of income to you while you give away the best hours of your day to that income. If you don't go to work and do what you need to do, you'll lose 100% of the income you're generating because you only have one cashflow.

On the flip side, if you're an employer—such as many small businesses—then you're controlled by the various burdens of that business (e.g., liabilities, franchise fees, various taxes and regulations, employees, and payroll). Very few small businesses have control over their livelihood and economic wellbeing. Between all these controlling elements, they feel like the business is running them and not the other way around. Very few people can remove themselves from the center of their businesses.

So, what is the success rate of a small business? About 80% of small businesses survive their first year. Of that, only 70% of those survive until the end of year two. And about half of those are still afloat at the end of year five.[2] These statistics ought to frighten anyone who's thinking about owning—or already owns—a business.

So, we know that most businesses will fail within the first few years, which is partly why we see so many people afraid to launch into business for themselves. Not to mention, according to Small Business Trends, only about 40% of small businesses turn a profit. Meanwhile, only 30% are breaking even and 30% are losing money.

It's hard for me to believe those numbers, frankly, but they're true. I actually estimate that a much larger percentage of companies are *not* turning a profit, based on how small businesses view what profit is. If those companies went through an audit and had their books thoroughly investigated—and adjusted—we'd probably find significantly less than 50% are actually turning a profit, which is beside the point.

The median household income in the United States was $67,521 in 2020. In 1989, the median income was $54,621, and those dollars went a lot further than they do today (due to price inflation).[3] That's a modest increase of only about $13,000 per year over almost twenty years.

If you go a step further and add race into the equation, the median incomes are even more telling—as noted below. For example, according to info collected by PBS from the Census Bureau, there's about a $41,000-per-year difference between Asian Americans and African Americans.[4]

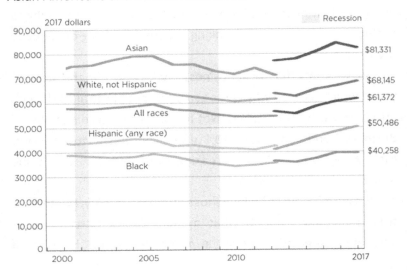

All that's to say that we know income stagnation is a very real thing. Why is that?

I'd posit there are multiple factors. I'm not going to say there aren't some systemic problems on the macro levels either. At the time I wrote this book, for example, we were having race protests all throughout the country after the death of an unarmed black man, George Floyd, who was killed at the hands of law enforcement.

Without chasing that rabbit too far down the hole, I think it's important to note that there are wage disparities that exist—and a lot of that disparity can be attributed to control (or lack thereof). This is not just a middle class problem. According to a November 19, 2022 article from MarketWatch, roughly 45% of those making more than $100,000 say they live paycheck to paycheck; 47% of those making between $150,000 to $200,000 a year; and 28% of those making over $200,000. So you see, individuals and families across the spectrum need more monthly passive income as they get their financial home in order.

As noted before, my goal is to elevate all people—regardless of race or ethnicity or other determining factors—to enter into this new paradigm where we are doing for ourselves so that we can do for others. If more people embarked upon this CFE lifestyle, we'd have far less poverty and wage stagnation.

In terms of investment, you're limited by the amount of time you can exchange for a return on your investment. When you're trading your time for money, there are only so many hours you can make that trade occur. That's why it's important to determine whether you are striving for active income, passive income, or both. Again, active income will require ongoing effort, and passive income will require ongoing capital (after the due diligence). However, the two are correlated in three ways:

1. The more passive income you earn, the more motivation you will have to increase your active income. You'll want to feed the beast.

2. The more passive income you earn, the more time you buy because there's less direct pressure to trade time for money.

3. Active income does not have to be your time traded for money. You can employ talent or outsource efforts to earn it. You could argue that this is a blend of both incomes.

At some point, you'll need to create some velocity with your income, start making some passive income, and leverage other people in their work so they can use their time to build your income streams. It's critical that you don't spend too much time in the goal-setting and planning phase. You need to jump right into action after you have a plan in place.

As they say, no man is an island. Notice they didn't mention you cannot be a rocket ship. Most folks, unfortunately, don't have the time or understanding of how to invest their money, so they will give it to Wall Street. It's a popular practice. The conceit is that the average investor—who probably doesn't know a whole lot about the fundamentals of market investing—believes that other people do know what they're doing. So, they trust others to make money for them.

The problem with that is they're abandoning what control they could have over their money and their future. Employers help this as well by offering 401k's that match employee contributions, and those funds are taken by financial managers to invest in various stocks, bonds, ETFs, or mutual funds.

Other people procure their own financial advisors, who tend to give you their own selection of funds they want you to invest in. You feel like you're picking because they give you a few options, but in the end, you're not really exercising freedom. It's within their constraints, and it's not usually what's best for you.

Sadly, most of these investments—let's just call them traditional investments—do not produce cashflow for the investor. They don't pay dividends (i.e., passive income), for example, at least in many cases, so that's something to be aware of. It's an *appreciation play* for most people.

You may know more about it than me if you're a seasoned investor, but I'm not a fan of the volatility and amount of risk inherent to the whole scene. It's a casino, and many people are taking cuts with your money.

And, to take us back to step 5, I much prefer assets that produce consistent and predictable income that I can trust. I just can't see getting there with stocks, bonds, funds and Wall Street in general.

The alternative for me would be to relinquish control and become an observer, which is what most people do. They watch what the stocks are doing. They don't always know why it's doing what it's doing. That lack of power is what Wall Street and the financial planners—Jim Kramer and the other nut jobs—want for you. They thrive in the chaos. If it's above your paygrade, they have job security. You put your money in, they penalize you if you take it out. The options they give you benefit them. They use a lot of jargon that's hard to understand, so you'll believe they're smarter than you.

That's the direct opposite of what I'm trying to do. I'm not trying to convince you I'm smarter than anyone else. I just know what I've seen work over nearly twenty years of working for myself. I've also made my share of mistakes along the way due to my learning curve and would love to help you avoid some of those.

My last attempt at Wall Street was in 2009. I had $10,000 in cash. Our museum exhibition company sold products to Freddie Mac. We saw their stock price go down to $3.25, and I told my wife, "They're a customer. I can't see them going any lower." So, we put $10,000 into Freddie Mac. I was driven based on emotion, and you may win that way from time to time in the short run, but in the long run, you will lose.

Shortly thereafter, the stock dropped below a dollar, then down to thirty-five cents, and I learned a tough lesson. Plus, my wife has teased me about the whole "Freddie Mac debacle" ever since, and I don't want to make that mistake again. It is a good practice to brainstorm on some bad investments you've made and why they didn't work out. I'd be willing to bet much was due to a lack of due diligence, control, and cashflow.

More and more people are setting up *self-directed IRAs*, and there are a number of different companies. You'll find a whole host of them out there. I'm not a financial adviser or tax adviser, so do your own research when setting up your retirement account. However, I can tell you that if you set up your self-directed IRA, you can invest in pretty much any asset type you want, such as a boat or house, as long as it's not your primary residence. You just have to be careful not to self-deal, which is when you use IRA funds to do business with yourself. You can also invest in businesses, stocks, or mortgage notes—the list is endless.

You can take control back by having the commitment and time to learn new asset classes and industries. You can find experts within those industries.

The CFE life requires this level of upfront planning and preparation, but the rewards are much more gratifying.

CHAPTER 5

The Win-Win Model

With great power comes great responsibility.
—Uncle Ben, Spider-Man

R uth and I sold our government contracting business in 2013 as an asset purchase sale, so we had turned that unexpected blessing into a handsome profit we would later leverage into a note investing business.

The thing is, we were totally burned out by that point, anyway. Had I continued down that path for much longer, I probably would have had a heart attack—or worse. My arms were buzzing all day long, and you'd often catch me off to the side massaging them to relieve the stress. What started off feeling freeing was starting to feel suffocating. We had looked down our noses at the corporate world and started our own company, and that was great.

However, we had clients from the Pentagon and all forms of leadership within the federal government. The project sizes were lofty, and the deadlines were strict. When you're dealing with an industry that involves both products and services, there are numerous ways for things to go wrong for you. And when you have a project that's as visible as museum exhibits and signage, for example, every little detail had to be perfect.

So, we listed our business with a broker and sold it within a year. The blessing was that we sold our business at its height and were able to take back a sizable business note. Plus, it gave me a chance to finally look at myself spiritually and in terms of my health.

I made some strict adjustments and focused on my next phase of life, which was a dedication to becoming a CFE and acting like a full-time investor as we built our next company. Chances are, your journey will look much different, and it's impossible to cover every situation. Still, know that the "who you are" is more important than the "what you do." What is your purpose in life? What is your mission? Is it that of a father or mother providing for your family? Or is it that of a young entrepreneur determining the best use of your time? You will need this understanding to motivate yourself as you make tough changes in your life, such as maintaining and reviewing your financial statement weekly.

I became a business owner initially to obtain freedom, but I found myself enslaved to the very thing that was supposed to give me that. I bought real estate properties that gave me more financial freedom, but it didn't yield quite enough cashflow to match my aspirations, so I decided to commit myself to a new goal.

I first thought it was about financial freedom. Later I thought it was about freedom of time. Now, I believe I'm serving society on a greater level with what I've learned how to do for myself.

I wanted to be able to do what I wanted when I wanted it, with whomever I wanted. And this became my battle cry: I would only buy assets I could control and where cash flowed. If it went outside these buying parameters, I wasn't interested. Later, I change my philosophy to assets that provide consistent income I can trust. This allowed me to move outside my comfort zone and learn to properly vet operators that can handle all the stresses of producing cash flow while I sleep at night.

This was further how I became a CFE. The goal was for this to carry me through the rest of my life. To not only be comfortable, but able to provide the kind of quality of life I felt my family deserved.

It tied into lessons I learned from childhood. I knew two discernible facts about myself. One, I'm a control freak. And two, I love earning money. It's not that I'm superficial, mind you. I believe I use these attributes to give back in greater ways.

That's because my goals aren't superficial. They have real meaning for me and the people I love.

What good is money if you can't bless the ones you love? So, that gets to the heart of what we're talking about herein.

My next journey was a foray into *mortgage note investing*—or real estate note investing. In a nutshell, I would buy notes that were in a distressed state and work with the borrower to get them to perform and, therefore, begin flowing cash. Notes being in a "distressed state" means the borrower hasn't made a payment in at least ninety days. You can purchase residential (homeowners) or commercial notes. I later found you can even do this with business notes, as well. The idea, however, is that it's a *win-win model.*

I'll elaborate.

Under my model, I'm able to help the sellers by buying notes they need to liquidate. I benefit myself by earning additional streams of income (from borrower payments). And I'm especially able to help the homeowners, who get terms they can afford so they can stay in their homes.

A lot of people don't understand that if they stop paying their mortgage, interest will still accrue on their account in the form of interest arrears. In many cases, there's a per diem interest accumulation of maybe ten dollars, for example, for every day they don't make a payment. Therefore, when they *do* start making payments, they can't just pick up from where they left off. They have to catch up with those interest arrears and any late fees on the account.

I was able to purchase the distressed notes at a discount, which gave me considerable flexibility when working with buyers. I could work out terms that fit their budget; hence, the win-win.

When you help someone get back on their feet with their mortgage, you're also improving the overall solvency of the neighborhood (i.e., the condition of the neighborhood) as well as the macro real-estate economy as a whole.

All these *adjustable-rate mortgages* underwriten in the 2000's really hindered our society. People were only getting a *fixed* interest rate for a year or two before it adjusted north. The lenders would underwrite the borrower on, let's say, a $300 monthly payment. They could look at their job, and their income and know what they could approve at that payment schedule. Those notes would then get securitized, pooled, and sold on the *secondary market*. Once the adjustable-rate hit after the fixed period ended, their payments would start going up to, say, $400 or $500—and the borrowers wouldn't be able to afford the spike.

Couple that with the financial crisis of 2008, and that's why we saw such an explosion in defaults and evictions once the bubble burst. People lost their jobs, and the rest is history.

If we were to go behind the scenes of your mortgage note, it might look like the following:

You see a mortgage as a way of buying a home, and it is. Investors see a mortgage as a stream of cash flow. These cash flows are originated, bought, sold, and securitized in secondary mortgage markets, which are incredibly large and liquid. From when your loan originates to when your monthly payments end up with an investor as part of a mortgage-backed security, asset-backed security, collateralized mortgage obligation, or collateralized debt obligation payment, various institutions carve out a percentage of the initial fees or monthly flows.

If you're new to mortgage note investing—or thinking about becoming an investor—there are four main participants in this market:

1. The mortgage originator
2. The aggregator
3. The securities dealer
4. The investor

I'm number four in this equation. Investors are the end-user of mortgages. You will find foreign governments, pensions, insurance companies, banks, hedge funds, large investors, and small investors buying and selling mortgage notes in secondary mortgage markets.

Most borrowers do not realize the extent to which their mortgage gets sliced, diced, and traded, and I cannot promise that it's always above board and good for the borrower.

But I set out with the mindset of helping the borrower; again, when everyone wins, it becomes more than a cold, calculated exchange. People must have a place to live, and sometimes the terms of their original loan aren't agreeable. Or those loans jump from fixed to adjustable at a certain point and that spike isn't sustainable.

However, the win-win model is sustainable.

I sometimes reflect on my life—as I've done herein—and realize I was at the perfect stage of my life to make sure this model became a great success.

Often, when people envision an investor, their minds automatically go to a man with a three-piece suit and slicked-back hair, who's posing in front of the giant bronze bull sculpture near Broadway and Wall Street. While that image is sometimes true, I think you'll find that it's a minority.

I knew this was my calling as soon as I got into it. I guess you could say—after Ruth and I sold the government contracting business and got into real estate mortgage notes— we were performing the first few brushstrokes of an all-new business model. One that I would not only do for myself but for others too. This was the point we finally started placing goals around our plan and creating something bigger than ourselves. Hence, the birth of the Win-Win Cycle.

First, you must have a clearly defined goal. You have to develop an action plan, and you have to master your fundamentals as you put that plan into place. Now, the fundamentals won't all be in place before executing, so let's get that out of our minds for now.

I wrote earlier that I read a lot of books before and during the early days, by authors such as Jim Rohn, Stephen Covey, J Scott, Robert Kiyosaki, Zig Ziglar, Bill Bartmann, and many others. But while I learned plenty from those masters, there's only so much you can find in any book. (And this is coming from a guy who just completed his fifth one!) Some things you must learn for yourself on the ground—as long as your mentality is right. Don't just go halfway. You have to go all in and really want to master your particular business model.

We'll talk about more of these concepts later.

To reiterate: *I'm on a mission to help every person in this world achieve more passive monthly income.*

The most important question is, how can you create a plan that's right for you? This is the question we'll be trying to answer throughout the remainder of this book.

It takes discipline (which doesn't magically rear its head) and creating a Win-Win Cycle for yourself. You'll want to put a diagram together of where you want to be within the next six months, one year, and five years. This is your *action plan* we will elaborate on a little bit further on! Your *battle cry*! It involves a clearly defined goal. It involves activity and execution. It involves learning fundamentals as you take those actions. It involves sharing what you've learned with other people. And it involves enhancing your action plan which feedback as the cycle repeats over and over.

The more I created my plan—and obsessed over it—the more my plans evolved over time. Each constituent part would feed off each other and keep evolving ad nauseum. Because one of my goals was freedom of time, I can attest that I've been much happier since.

Most people manage to start with goal setting. They may even put together an action plan, but they never make it past the execution stage. It may be because of fear. It could be because they don't feel they know enough. They lack confidence or feel like they don't have enough guidance. They may not feel they're smart enough. Whatever the case may be, there's some type of perceived inadequacy there. There's a missing piece, so the plan falls apart.

They worry so much about failure that they attract failure to themselves. I don't know if you've ever heard of the law of attraction, but the concept is the same. Essentially states that if you want to receive positive energy from the universe, you have to put out positive energy (i.e., like attracts like). So, that's the problem with constantly harping on the negative. Just like you can attract positive energies from the universe, you can also attract negative energies (heartache, sickness, pain, setbacks, etc.).

Create goals. Create an action plan which will deliver you your goals and make sure it's in alignment with your identity. Get consumed by the action plan. Morning, noon, and night, think about that plan and get the creative juices going. Then start executing in tangible ways. For example, as you're meeting with people and self-educating, start to venture out and take forward-moving action. As you do that, you'll learn the fundamentals of that industry.

At the same time, you have to make sure your goals are aligned with your values. For some, this may mean connecting with others that hold similar values and have shown themselves to be financially successful. You can then find out what their goals and action plans have been and adjust accordingly.

It's not going to be easy, so you have to get consumed by the process. As you do, you'll start forming daily rituals that take years to cultivate. And I can tell you, even though I've been immersed in my industry for years, I'm still cultivating those habits. But it all starts with getting consumed.

Working the Win-Win Cycle while you build an entrepreneurial life first requires all the important areas of your life to be evaluated. As it relates to goal setting, I think of this as the Five Cs.

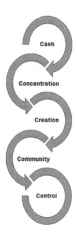

This is a great way to start building your goals and plans. They all run concurrently, so it's not that you start with cash, then go to the community, and so on. It all runs at the same time.

Even so, everything starts with **Cash**. As we discussed earlier, you need to understand your financial situation and have a sense of your future financial situation before you can move forward. This is not to say you will create additional streams of income from your capital reserves. Some of my most lucrative opportunities were the results of who I knew and what I knew, as opposed to a capital outlay. Either way, at some point down your CFE journey, you will need some cash as you invest in yourself.

As for **Concentration**, take time to reflect on all the areas you have control of and all the things you need to take control of. What have you done to take control of these areas and why did you take the initiative to do so? What happened in the areas you lost control over? Ponder this question until you understand the road you've taken and why.

Now, let's look at several additional questions to ponder (before examining the following model):

- Have you reached rock bottom?
- Why this industry and not another?
- Why do you want additional streams of income?
- Why did you pick up this book?
- Why do you want to be a CFE?
- Do you want more possessions?
- Do you want more security for yourself and your family?
- Is it because you're curious or are you already there, trying to enhance your operation?
- What has led you to this point?

After reviewing the example above, feel free to start mind-mapping the individual details of your plan. Don't worry. A mind-map is not a complex concept; it's a basic diagram to visually organize your thoughts. Typically, like the example above, it's hierarchical in nature and reflects the various relationships between the different pieces of information. You'll often see a single image in the center with associated representations, images, words, or parts of words added. Major ideas relate to the central concept, and ideas branch out from the center.

I've grown accustomed to using the *Xmind* software tool to make my mind-maps. There are some other options out there, but Xmind is easy to use, and you can buy it outright at the time I am writing this. Many software programs require you to pay an ongoing subscription fee, but for Xmind you can pay $129 upfront, which is what I prefer to do. Notice to this point of going through steps 1 through 3, this is the first mention of having to spend money yet many folks never get this far.

When I use Xmind, I think about what my strengths and weaknesses are. Begin by thinking about the investment you're looking at, the opportunity you're considering, or the goal you're contemplating. That will go at the center, and ideas relating to the main concept will branch out from there. For example, when you start to build out your plan—with a support team or strategic partnerships—it'll be good to know what you need to hire out for and what you can do yourself.

As you look to bring on partners or form relationships, everything is best done in baby steps. I think of strategic partnerships like dating. You don't go on a first date and ask them to marry you right away. You maybe take them to a movie or dinner and have good conversation, then repeat. You get to know them over time and see how that relationship evolves. Things feel right because there's this whole organic flow to it.

This is also true of the mentor-mentee dynamic. A lot of people wrongly look at the mentor-mentee dynamic as being tantamount to a student-teacher dynamic; however, that couldn't be further from the case. Often, a mentor-mentee relationship actually looks closer to mentor-mentor.

Do you recognize what a huge difference that slight wording change translates into?

When you're looking at people to partner with or take on as a mentor, it's good to fully understand what you bring to the table and what you lack. I think the best relationship, no matter what section of the value chain you're in, is when you match your strengths with someone else's weaknesses.

When my former company worked with the Pentagon, I matched my strength with the government's weakness. Simply put, they didn't have the desire or capability to design and fabricate an exhibit like we could, so that's something I could do. But, on the other hand, my weakness was cashflow. I had to keep money coming through the door to pay for our ongoing operation, so that was very important for us. It was the Pentagon; they had plenty of financial resources.

So, think about it in terms of opportunity. Their strengths and weaknesses and your own. If you approach relationships that way, you'll be able to come from a much stronger position.

To those ends, what is your current financial situation?

That's very important to look at because, for example, you may not need to run out and quit your job to become a full-time note investor right away. In fact, you'd be giving up a stream of income if you did that, and that's something I rarely advise. That runs very contrary to my goals and objectives, as I'm always looking to add streams of income. Keep your job. Figure out how to bring more value to your employer so you can be rewarded over time. You should be looking at additional streams of income outside that, not a job replacement.

Do you have a current financial plan? Step 1 covered creating and maintaining a living financial statement that you review weekly, but how can you build your financial goals into your statement and convert it to a key performance indicator? Over time, you measure your performance toward meeting you goals and course correct as needed.

The **Creation** phase of the Five Cs comes next. This involves building an action plan to gain control over areas you've lost it (this is also how you start gaining the fundamentals needed to start achieving the freedom of time you're seeking). We will explore strategies for creating additional streams of income in the next chapter, but they'll come from your own unique situation.

Or maybe your goals are different. I've established that I wanted to be a CFE with numerous streams of income and freedom of time.

At the end of the day, you're responsible for your own goals and actions despite some circumstances that may occur outside your control. Whether set backs occur because of you or otherwise, the strength of your discipline needs to propel you forward.

You might say, "I don't have the money," or "I don't have the time." Sometimes that actually means, "I don't have the mindset." Or it may involve your commitment or your fundamentals.

It's not that you don't have the money.

For people who invest and commit, money finds them. As for time, refer to the outreach matrix. You can adjust it to help with time management and productivity or use some of the free planning tools that are everywhere nowadays (e.g., Trello, Slack, Google Drive). You will be amazed at how you can create time that wasn't there before. Slack, for example, is a cloud-based collaboration tool that enables users to chat one-on-one or in groups and share documents. Now, it began as a communication tool but gained its currency among various enterprises and broadened into a collaboration platform with capabilities that go beyond messaging.

I've seen that happen time and time again. The most successful investors I've known started with very little capital. I've also seen investors start with a few million (which isn't the norm), and they're nowhere near as successful now as some of the ones who started with much less.

In my case, I started out with $240,000 in capital (with a high-interest loan), selling a product I didn't know in an industry I didn't understand. But I did it anyway, and I learned as I went, so I suggest learning and doing through the creation and execution of an action plan. Worry about the money later!

Let's talk about **Community**, the next of the Five Cs, before doubling back to control. Community is all about who needs to be with you on your journey (on both a macro and micro level). I suggest starting small with an inner circle.

You have to be very strategic, which involves a lot of planning and committed use of the outreach matrix. On a micro level, some people are going to be the closest to you. They will affect you the most, and you will have the most impact on their lives. You will help each other reach your goals. Start with these individuals and grow your way out to the macro level.

On the macro level, as you grow, you become an influencer in the community as someone with integrity and, eventually, thought leadership, which should be the end goal.

Who are these people who should be in your inner circle? As noted, it involves a lot of research. For that, I suggest using LinkedIn. Sales Navigator is a tool you have to pay for, but it allows you to research people and gives you unlimited connections throughout that platform. Most of the business community is on LinkedIn, so if you're not on there yet I'd highly suggest it. On LinkedIn, there should be a 3:1 ratio when researching the people you need to connect with. For example,

I'd spend three hours trying to find the right people and then an hour trying to build a relationship with them. This is especially useful when you're first starting out. Once you've been in the industry a while, however, you'll start to line things out naturally. You'll understand who the thought leaders are, the connectors, the people you need to reach out to and hopefully bring into your own circle. But you're going to have to put in some sweat.

Set up a routine and manage expectations. You really need to have a work schedule for yourself, which is where the expectations come in. What needs to be done? You have your action plan, so how do you execute these steps every day?

As I'm writing this book, I have four young children who are eight and under, and I see my children more than most fathers. I operate a $50 million dollar income fund with my partner. I run a sizable collection business on top of the fund. I manage a portfolio of commercial and residential properties my wife and I own. I write books every other year.

I have to make time for what's important to me, just like you'll have to do if you're serious about building additional streams of income. Everything I do involves surrounding myself with the right people and being prepared for opportunities before they present themselves. Being prepared, having the right community, and staying focused will take you far in life.

To put it another way, if something is a priority, you'll make time for it. And if you have a pain point, you'll be even more likely to find the time. Now, if you're not at that pain point or if it's not that important if it happens, then it's not going to unfold the way you want it to unfold.

You know the steps of your action plan, so commit to some daily actions to ensure those things happen. As the momentum builds, so do the fundamentals.

I also suggest as you start building your plan out. Use tools like Zoom once you establish your contacts and grow your network. You can make deeper connections that way, and there are collaborative tools like Slack that are pretty much like Facebook but in a more private setting. If you build a strategic partner network, for example, you can do weekly calls and masterminds, which are things I enjoy, myself. You can use https://doodle.com/ to coordinate meetups in an efficient manner.

Time is your most precious resource, so be aware of time bandits (people who would waste your time). Surround yourself with individuals who will make you better and who you will make better, and weed out the ones who don't bring you value.

You have the **Control** to make this change as it comes to your community, which is the last C. To have control means "to have the power to run something in an orderly way."[5] Your control over your life and your actions determines your level of discipline, which is needed for effective execution.

I've learned to embrace my control freak without letting it completely overtake me (no easy task at times). I figured out all the areas of my life I needed to take control of, then did something about it. And now, you are one step closer to identifying the areas you need to take control of.

Let's discuss some strategies for creating multiple streams of income.

CHAPTER 6

Learning to Execute

Ideas don't make you rich. The correct execution of ideas does.

—Felix Dennis

As you continue to attempt to execute your action plan, you will begin to understand all the additional resources needed to have success. That's where mind-mapping becomes important for me.

Capital is one big consideration for any CFE, and the more you have of it the less effort you may need to exert. I always start with people I'm mentoring by asking them about their *financial statement*, as I've mentioned about a thousand times now. Do you have a financial statement with all your business activities? Or is that something you need to work on? Remember, you can email me at martin@2cfnow.com and I'll send you a living financial statement template you can use.

Your income statement should show *income* and *expenses* and a balance sheet with all your *assets* and *liabilities*. I host my statements on Google Drive so my wife and I both have access.

For my income statement, I do the following each month:

1. I have a section for my active income and a section for my passive income. On the far right of the spreadsheet, it totals the passive income and compares it to my passive income goal. For example, if my monthly passive income goal is $200,000, and my actual monthly income totals $100,000, I'm 50% the way there and know I need to get back to work. I have my passive income further broken down into categories of earning methods, such as notes, real estate landlording, royalties, and limited partnerships.

2. In the expense section, I break out living expenses and expenses to run my businesses. I want to understand how my passive income would match up to my living expenses if my business disappeared overnight.

3. I then look at my monthly cashflow by subtracting total income by total expenses.

4. I also have a few metrics in this section. I strive for the 40/40/20 rule, which states that 40% of your income should be set aside for investing, 40% should be set aside for taxes, and you should live off 20% of your income. If that 20% isn't enough to cover your living expenses, then it is your responsibility to earn more income. I also toy

with the idea of doing a sub-breakout for investing into categories of cash storage, further cashflow investing, and the purchase of precious metals.

For the balance statement, I do the following for each month:

1. For assets, I divide everything into banking, passive investments, real estate, notes, and others. I want to understand the different categories of my portfolio so I can study each one independently. For the "other" category, I put down assets such as precious metals, Bitcoin, Bitcoin mining, and vehicles. I prefer having two sections for my asset column: one for income producing assets and one for store of value assets. I consider a store of value asset as an asset, commodity, or currency that can be saved, retrieved, and exchanged in the future without detereriorating in value.

2. For liabilities, I break down current liabilities and long-term liabilities. My debt is mainly tied to income-producing assets such as real estate. I'm careful not to take on bad debt that doesn't advance my income. *Rich Dad* taught me well.

Each week, each month, most of your numbers will change. Some figures remain constant, like fixed income, mortgage payments, and taxes, but the rest will likely change. I recommend setting up your financial statement so you compare month to month and study any variances. To help with quick access to data, I have a password-protected Excel file. I then have all my account login pages in an organized folder system on Google Chrome. I go through each account and pull down the information once a week. Then, my wife and I meet weekly to discuss our current standing, how far we are from our goals, and moves we can make to advance. We also can observe trends, both good and bad, that are externally driven but need to be understood just the same. The more income you earn and the further distance you gain from your living expenses, the less negative trends (such as any increases in living expenses) will affect your movement.

Even if you're in the beginning stages of becoming a CFE, you should still build your statement for how things will look down the road. For example, let's say you have one rental property, and your goal is to have ten properties by the end of the year. You can place a stakeholder for rental property #2 all the way to #10 as a motivator to help get you there.

Furthermore, you can use financial software such as QuickBooks. On my business side, I've been using QuickBooks Online for years. All my accounts feed into it, and I have my bookkeeper reconcile my books monthly while producing management reports.

On the passive income front, everything really begins with the acquisition of assets that produce income while possibly creating expenses. This may carry liability, depending on if you take on leverage, use existing capital, or give away equity. On the active income side, it's possible that you trade additional time for money, and nothing hits liability, assets, or expenses.

What are your objectives financially? Put some thought into your skillsets and what resources you need to achieve your objectives. Needing resources doesn't always mean you should purchase them. Instead, it could mean forming a strategic partnership with someone who has those resources or giving some of your equity position away if you're controlling the deal. The important thing is to get a handle on the resources needed to achieve your goals and how they will affect your financial statement and time management.

You can think of resources in terms of physical and non-physical. Physical resources could be tools or computers, for example. Non-physical resources are things like software or cloud-based support systems like Google Drive, Dropbox, and Podio.

As for labor, do you have your children or spouse to help you move forward? Chore charts are something to institute with younger children to make sure they're learning the right habits early on. If they're a little older, maybe they can be a good partner or hourly employee.

When you run a company with your spouse, you either become much closer or drift further apart. Hopefully, you can make it a bonding experience like my wife and I did. I have been very fortunate.

What resources do you need to obtain? In other words, what money, materials, staff, network, or other assets do you need to draw on achieve your objective? I recommend using Xmind to mind map the answers. Perhaps start with the categories mentioned above and itemize the answers. Then tie all the resource categories into your financial statement and time management setup. You can make projections of how your financial statement and time management set will look to achieve your action plan obligations.

That's a significant question. I hope you can answer it definitively by the end of this book. It's a critical question that will make or break your execution.

The important thing to note is that how you procure resources will tie directly into the people you need to be networking with.

To recap, we made exhibits for the federal government. They weren't capable of fabricating exhibits themselves. But they gave us what we needed, which was cash, in exchange for what they needed, which was exhibit displays. The same concept will apply to note investing or any other opportunity that holds the potential for additional streams of income. You need to know what resources are needed to succeed for every opportunity. You need to know which ones you currently have and which ones you do not. And you need to network strategically according to your strengths and weaknesses.

Once you have your action plan together, I recommend posting it somewhere, whether it's on a computer or printed on paper. Also, you'll want to follow your metrics closely, which will reflect how well you're executing your plan. Post your metrics on your bathroom mirror or your computer or in your office on a whiteboard. I like the whiteboard method, myself. They're a great way to keep track of your activities in a more tangible way as well as quotes, goals, and/or metrics.

I have whiteboards everywhere and track a range of metrics, including how my action plan is going, how the notes are performing (in terms of people paying and not paying), who's paying me off and at what time, who I'm reaching out to, how my capital raise goals are tracking. We also have quotes that run throughout the office that are customer-focused, sales-focused, and motivational.

You're about 42% more likely to achieve your goals if you write them down.[6] I think the entirety of the 42% who achieve their goals have one thing in common: discipline. Without discipline, execution is improbable if not altogether impossible. It's not just writing your goals down. It's executing a plan to achieve your goals. Writing them down simply serves as a continuous reminder and affirmation.

Unfortunately, most people fail to take control of their lives, which is the number one reason why most people cannot execute their plans.

Over my seventeen years in business, I've seen people fail to take back control when starting businesses and investing. The second biggest reason people fail at execution is a lack of discipline. It's tough for many because we live in a world that encourages mediocrity.

To form the discipline through all the previous steps such as having a work schedule and managing the time within those schedules . . . that, right there, is true commitment!

People think of commitment like, "Let me go commit to doing this for you or me." But commitment is something that happens on the back end, after you've shown discipline over time. So, commitment is the result of showcasing your discipline and self-control.

You also must keep the energy level up. I see this as a big problem in today's society—the lack of energy. There's no intensity. For many people, they haven't hit the right pain point or feel uncomfortable enough in their current situation to want to become the catalyst for change.

Complacency sets in. There's a general lack of self-control. There's a total loss of energy. Discipline is out the window. The CFE lifestyle is merely a catchy tagline with no purpose or direction. And there's no self-control.

Keep in mind, I say "self" because there's always control, whether you're the one with it or someone or something else is, as noted earlier. In other words, just because you're not in control, just because you're not executing, doesn't mean there's no control. It just means you're not the one with it.

If that's the case, who is? We'll marinate on that one for a little bit as we pivot to looking at your plan.

As you develop and execute your action plan, you will start gaining more and more power. You will feel stronger and more confident as you move forward. Just taking ownership of your situation for the first time in a long time will add to your motivation. The first step to building an action plan is to prepare. You can incorporate the five steps into your preparation. In the end, what needs to be accomplished to achieve a CFE lifestyle? Second, what needs to get implemented and how? You can use the outreach matrix, Trello, Xmind, Slack, and a number of tools to help you map and carry out your action plan.

The main component is an accountability partner to keep you on track. In have my wife, business coach, business partners, and a higher power—to name a few partners in my life.

Last, who is taking ownership of what needs to be implemented? Call this all out in your plan for each activity needed. I recommend scheduling blocks of time in your weekly schedule to flush things out and implement activities.

Just like you may have a schedule at your job—let's say 9:00 a.m. to 5:00 p.m.—you would also commit blocks of time to this new business, new opportunity, or new investment. You will then schedule how you're going to use that time during those blocks as you go through, day by day.

Most people will not do this, usually unaware that they should be. I think they somehow fail to grasp the power they have in their own hands. Most people are driven by emotion. The more they experience good things in life, the more time and resources they dedicate to that thing. For example, if your relationship is going well, then you're feeling good and you keep pouring back into that relationship. Or maybe your job is going well and you're riding a wave of emotions and keep reinvesting yourself back into your job.

It's not that doubling down on things you're good at is inherently wrong. It's just that—on the other hand—it's too easy to ignore the things we aren't doing well in. We don't want to think about our shortcomings because the emotions are negative and we seek to avoid them altogether.

Sometimes things like hard work or frustration throw people off as well, so they try to avoid that. And the execution phase— or fear of the frustrations that may come from it—serves as a blocker.

Part of forming a CFE life is to build time schedules for when you work on things per your action plan instead of focusing on what drives you emotionally. So, you want to treat this as your job—or your mission. Think about it as a necessity. This will require you to focus on areas of weaknesses and procrastination. I've found that some people won't know their weaknesses but are much quicker to find those areas where they procrastinate (and those are weaknesses too).

Remember, procrastination is the result of something you're weak at. Knowing that is important. When you're scheduling the activities you're weak at, do those first. Get them out of the way, then the whole rest of your day is going to be much easier for you.

Benjamin Franklin once said, regarding procrastination, "You may delay but time will not."[7] So, time keeps on ticking away whether we're moving forward, standing still, or going backward. And I think most people would agree that the only way to keep from moving backward (or being complacent) is to focus on those procrastination areas and move forward.

How do we do that?

One method is to let your spouse or significant other have access to your schedule, so they know you have certain times you need to be alone to build out the phases of your plan.

One of the hardest parts of working on something new is how much isolation you need. You must be able to concentrate on what you're trying to put together. There are always other people vying for your time, which is why I suggest posting your schedule where they can see it. They can see what you're up to and what kind of time is involved, so it's a good tactic to bring in supportive people.

Maybe there are certain tasks on which you need to coordinate with others, so you can use some type of shared resources like Google Drive or Dropbox. Podio is another good project management system. It's cloud-based and enables you to assign and/or share tasks with one another.

Make sure anyone you bring into your inner circle is a positive influence, whether they're virtual assistants or independent contractors or direct employees. Surrounding yourself with positive, uplifting people—as opposed to time bandits or people who would tear you down—will help you with accountability and staying on task. They can often be very motivational as well. For example, my energy level is naturally pretty high. However, if I were to allow myself to associate with people who were a drag on my energy level then eventually I'd be affected.

Thinking back to my museum exhibition company, my wife and I brought on a designer that was—simply put—exceptional. Doing this allowed us to make sure our projects had quality and integrity. The construction end of our business was top notch, so that was good. At the same time, his attitude was very negative. He was a prima donna. We always had to cater to his mood swings. Believe it or not, we put up with that for about three years, and that was a mistake. I would never do anything like that again.

As an employer or someone who's paying for a service, you should expect the people you surround yourself with to work within your culture of positivity and high energy.

Now, you will have to cut out areas of your life that aren't growing to fit your schedule. Make a list of activities that don't bring you value or lead you away from your goals and do some trimming.

The main determining factor in whether you become a CFE is your commitment. It's your commitment that determines whether you can accomplish the goals you've established. You can have more than one goal, but start with things that bring you value—and make sure you're working efficiently inside those time blocks.

One thing I've done for over twenty years is planning my next day. At the end of each day, I plan out tomorrow. The cycle repeats. It has become a habit; I don't think I could stop doing this if I tried.

Having a planner is a good idea, and you can use that to plan out your next day too. Think about all the tasks you want to accomplish—and be detailed. I think you'll find that it'll keep you on time and help keep out those things that might be a drain (like time bandits or distractions).

When I was a mortgage officer, I used to plan all my calls for the next day before the end of the day. I'd assemble a call list before going home (making sure I had all the appropriate names and numbers) and then jot out some notes regarding what I wanted to talk about. This was before iPhones, so I'd just staple business cards to a piece of paper and write notes out on the side of each card. It was very rudimentary but served its purpose for a time.

I attribute that one habit to being able to become the second-highest-producing mortgage officer out of roughly 700 peers. Mapping out my day before it happened meant I could go right into the tasks at hand and be uber-productive the next day.

The key is to be massively productive by treating your time like gold. When you're a CFE you don't have "filler time." You don't have downtime. So, I can't stress enough the importance of control, which should be translated into planning your various day-to-day actions.

I use Grant Cardone's 10X Planner and write in my task lists under the "hourly schedule" section. I write down my daily goals the day prior. I use a quote for the day—my daily battle cry, if you will. I also write out my daily goals as if I've already accomplished them. For example:

- I raised $10,000.
- I made ten new contacts.
- I established one new cashflow stream.
- I was super patient with my family.

I'm affirming that those goals are already accomplished and then checking them off one by one as I go. If, by chance, a particular goal isn't handled on the right day, that goal would be rolled over into the next day. It's always better when you take your goals and morph them into daily positive affirmations because it's a self-fulfilling practice that can be made a habit over time.

My quote of the day might be something like, "I"m going to crush it today!" Or it might be, "My God is moving mountains today."

For targets, I might focus on investors for a capital raise or I might list my family. For successes, I just write down some things that I accomplished

The 10X Planner has turned into my journal, more or less, and I highly suggest giving it a try. It will help you stay focused on your action plans and goals, butt make sure you also use an online calendar so other can acknowledge your time blocks.

As I get through items during the day I'll cross them off which always feels good. Keep in mind, even if you're the most dedicated planner, you're going to be tested by your own mind. The more structure you have around your day, the better prepared you'll be to fight those demons. Tasks become habits, and I've found there's a whole spiritual element to constantly accomplishing things.

To get to the point where you can also go from control to full control, what are some things that need to change? And how do we execute better? These are some of the questions we'll discuss in the following chapter. In the meantime, I'd like to share some images from my career with you.

IMAGE GALLERY

#1: Our first government contract. The POW MIA
Memorial is still on display at the Pentagon.

#2: The POW MIA exhibit at the Pentagon.

#3: Our company designed, fabricated, and installed various display cases, panels, and map grid displays.

#4: A large exhibit our company designed,
fabricated, and installed.

#5: Our company provided an exhibit center
honoring General Colin Powell.

#6: Spending quality time with my first mentor, Marty Granoff, in Fort Lauderdale, FL, in 2020. We performed numerous deals, and I cherish everything he taught me.

#7: My first note-investing speaking engagement in Washington DC in 2017.

#8: My first note-investing speaking engagement in Washington DC in 2017 (continued).

#9: My protégé group's dinner in 2020.

#10: Time spent at the Pentagon with friend, Chaim Ekstein

#11: My Bequest babies showing up for a conference event

#12: My business partner, Shawn Muneio,
and myself at a Bequest Charity Event

CHAPTER 7

The Fundamentals of Your Plan

Faith is the substance of things hoped for, the evidence of things not seen.

—Hebrews 11:1

The goal of living as a CFE is to take control back over your life, which requires some faith on your part. You may feel like your faith isn't strong right now. I hope the tips I've laid out help you envision what your life could look like given the right action steps.

Take a look at the quote that opened this chapter. The truth is, the act of acquiring fundamentals comes through our daily activities and the execution of our plans. In other words, don't allow a lack of anything—in business or spiritually—to prevent you from taking action.

It won't happen overnight. It won't happen at all without matching action to your faith (and executing your plan). But . . .

The more streams of income you have, especially on a passive level, the less you are controlled!

The mastery will come as you plan and execute accordingly, but it all boils down to taking action to get to the point where you can learn the fundamentals.

Action-planning and mind-mapping are two of the biggest contributors to my success. However, when I'm taking on a new protégé who's all amped up and excited to begin building additional streams of income, they sometimes believe they need to acquire all the fundamentals of their plan before executing. In fact, if asked, most of them would probably say that the fundamentals have to come before the execution. I think that's another reason why so many people end up failing.

If you plan correctly, you can start building your fundamentals within your business or opportunity, as you're making your first moves toward the CFE lifestyle. This entails making a ton of mistakes, of course, and having some hard days, but these mistakes will ultimately be worth their weight in gold.

The first ten real estate notes I purchased were some real dogs. I mean, they were really bad. I spent about $240,000 to buy them. I thought I had done a good job with my *due diligence*, but I overlooked certain aspects of that process that would have informed me not to buy those notes.

So, what happened? Well, for starters, I did lose some money on my first purchase. Even so, I got some much-needed schooling on the fundamentals of note investing, which helped me with my next purchase.

Often, people will stick their toe in the water and get bitten right away—which is what holds them back. After that, they very quickly decide that they're not going to jump back into the water. So, the execution falls all apart.

Yes, I may have taken some hard hits up front. Yes, I wish I'd had better fundamentals to cut down on my learning curve, but it's never too late to get those. And in your case, we can help you to cut down on that learning curve. It's still going to require action, however.

Even though I made some mistakes early on, I lived to fight another day and to make a second purchase, a third, and so on. In other words, when my toe got nibbled, I didn't pull back and stop. I was bound and determined to execute, and I picked up the fundamentals as I went along. Here I am today, with well over a thousand notes purchased in the past seven years as a full-time note investor.

The number of streams you can acquire is only limited by your commitment and study of your industry. Moreover, it requires a lifelong commitment to learning about the industry and asset types (i.e., *asset classes*) from which you will derive your streams of income.

Recall your days as a student. What did you do? You probably took copious notes. When prompted, you regurgitated those notes back, and there wasn't a whole lot of creativity involved (unless it was an essay-type assignment, for example).

Now think about your career as an investor or would-be investor today. You should be taking notes (journaling) every day, especially early in your career. Journaling will show you the road you're paving for yourself and help you figure out how to move forward. If you ever decide to write a book, journaling will polish those skills over the years, as well. The story is already laid out too.

The idea is to be a student again—a student of your craft and industry. As you're learning and executing, journaling will help you to enhance those skills, uncover strengths and weaknesses, and plot your course of action. This is the heart of step 3 where you are researching additional streams of income.

Unlike my journey with notes, you probably have some expertise in some area you would like to explore for additional streams of income. You may already have the fundamentals mapped out and just need to document them. This will help you as you build yourself into communities and determine how to monetize things. Or make some training videos, write a book, or commit to some other way of creating a stream.

I recommend first documenting what you know before you research how to use your knowledge to advance yourself.

1. Think about who you need to connect with and why.

2. What holes or weaknesses need plugging to deliver a strong offer to the marketplace?

3. How can you leverage your existing strengths?

As I mentioned before, I went to community college before going on to receive my bachelor's degree and then two master's degrees. Had you told me then that I would not only go to college but enjoy it, I would called you were crazy. I just wasn't a good student in the traditional sense because—as I later learned—I was a control freak and traditional education was not the right format for me.

It took college and the right professor to allow me some flexibility to really spread my wings and fly (pardon the cliché). Once I graduated, I didn't quit being a student.

You shouldn't either.

No matter what age you are, you should be a lifelong student of your craft, your industry, and all the necessary skills involved. It will help if you map out the flow of your tasks each day and create various categories in a personalized *operations manual*. This allows you to have systems in place that allow for scalability, which translates into obtaining more streams of income from an industry once you crack that nut.

You'll find that the manual's layout tends to dictate its usability, so being as organized as possible is key.

1. Begin with an outline by dividing your manual into sections that coincide with the internal organization of your company. This will facilitate employee contributions

(if applicable) and allow easy access to information once it's complete.

2. Include a table of contents.

3. Make sure you or whoever helps author your manual use the same word-processing software, which will make it easier to construct and ensure the document can be easily modified in the future (pro tip: always keep a hard copy of all the versions in a safe location).

4. Number the sections and pages within each section. For example, page 3 of section 9 would be numbered "3.9" This will save you from having to reprint the entire document every time you make a change. Popular word-processing programs typically provide this option.

5. On each page, consider adding a footer that indicates when the page was last modified. Photocopied pages frequently lie around, and an outdated one could do a lot of damage.

6. Include an appendix for additions or changes so you won't have to edit or reprint the manual to include the occasional alterations.

7. Follow the model of most manuals: utilize four basic types of information, including how-to procedures (e.g., how to enter a new account into your CRM), locations of items, contacts, and various business-related policies.

Not everyone is a writer, so don't feel bad if your operations manual isn't as detailed as mine or others'. But there are several examples online, so you can do some research to see what works best for you. At the end of the day, it's about treating your CFE experience as seriously as your business—because it is.

If you place heavy emphasis on *sourcing* new cashflow stream opportunities, for example, you will eventually work toward receiving off-the-street opportunities. You don't just find customers where a normal business finds customers (real-estate note investing is very niche). You have to be way more targeted. In short, if you make yourself a student of sourcing, you will accomplish that. You will have excellent fundamentals for that aspect of your business.

Sourcing starts with *identity*. Earlier, we discussed having a mission statement. We noted my mission statement. You also need a marketing brand (i.e., identity) that allows you to become a magnet for cash-flowing assets. In this way, they can find you on an ongoing basis, and you don't have to exert your time and energy finding them.

Imagine if you don't work on your identity. You'll end up spending ongoing amounts of energy on finding opportunities, those opportunities aren't going to be at retail pricing, and the customers aren't going to be well-targeted customers. All the energy you exerted on servicing the wrong customers or assets will be wasted. You need to be taking in the right assets and customers with a magnetic effect that comes from underwriting the opportunity business or investment.

Underwriting means you're vetting an opportunity to better understand the value of that opportunity. But before underwriting can begin, you must consider what resources you need to vet the opportunity.

For instance, you may need to employ certain vendors to give you reports that are necessary to underwrite the opportunity. In my industry, we use resources that allow us to pull credit, skip trace, and obtain county records and property valuations.

So, the way you underwrite your opportunities will go hand-in-hand with your *mission statement* and require a lot of diligence and planning.

What resources do you need to properly underwrite your potential stream of income? It's critical to look at three risk factors:

1. *Operator*. What experience does the operator have? How much skin do they have in the game financially? What is their time commitment for the opportunity? Will they pass a background check? Is there any operator oversight, such as a third-party administrator or oversight organization?

I can't tell you the number of times I've come across individuals who have invested in an opportunity with an operator who was incompetent, didn't have any money in the fund themselves, or wouldn't pass a background check. There was one fund operator that worked a full-time job and operated the fund as a side hustle. This person had no money in the fund themselves, yet pounded social media with how wonderful they were. Talk about a train wreck waiting to happen!

2. *Capital Preservation*. How will the operator and business opportunity protect your capital?

It's important to understand all the internal and external risk factors that could lose your money. You want to know how the operator performs due diligence on cash-flowing assets and the key performance indicators in place to ensure ongoing control as they manage the portfolio. It's also important to understand external factors and their probability of occurring. How does the reward match up to the risk? This is why building yourself into a community within the industry is a good idea. You can get some outside perspectives on opportunities which will allow you to better measure the current opportunity against other potentially better ones. This is referred to as an opportunity cost.

On another note, the more you understand the asset class based on your experience, research and passion, the more you will better understand the operator and their ability to perform due diligence on assets while managing the assets to their optimum performance.

3. *Cashflow*. Does the cashflow meet your financial expectations or requirements? What is the time commitment period for the opportunity and is it in line with your plan to build wealth? Is the cashflow worth the risk?

You always hear stories of investments with very high returns. Yet, like in a casino, you never hear as much about the times folks get hammered on a deal. I know that most think about an annual return on an investment, but let me mention the importance of the monthly passive income the opportunity spits out. If you have a conservative opportunity that's paying out an annual preferred return of 8% and makes distributions monthly, you have predictability with that investment. You know that if you can manage to invest $100,000, you will receive $667 per month in cashflow (assuming no fees). The 8% won't retire you, but it may free you up to focus on generating greater incomes elsewhere. It becomes a time allocation factor.

Time commitment comes into play because there's a risk to interest rate if inflation drives past your fixed return rate. You don't want to be locked into a long-term deal. You want liquidity so you can pull your funds and place them in another vehicle that meets your adjusted financial goal.

You may be thinking that these are the type of questions that can only be answered once an opportunity presents itself, but that couldn't be further from the truth. To piggyback off our tips concerning proper planning and due diligence, you can actually be prepared to underwrite your new opportunities *before* they present themselves.

That's a big difference!

You need to be ready to receive an opportunity before it presents itself to you. This is just good due diligence.

Who in the industry do you need to connect with to get you where you're going? Think in terms of vendors, industry experts, sellers, customers, peers, and the (often overlooked) people who used to be in the industry but aren't anymore—who are often your most valuable allies. They may, in fact, have assets you can buy if they're no longer actively involved or looking to downsize. Or they may be able to give you certain resources you can use without any bias. Years ago, I ran into a landlord that got his residential rental properties by doing a mail-out campaign to landlords that had moved out of his state. This was brilliant because landlords that moved out tended to become emotionally disconnected from their properties and wanted to offload them.

Next, form a *pricing formula* to help you properly price the asset so it delivers the right *return expectation*.

If you're a newbie and don't know the parameters or fundamentals within the industry, it's important to get a mentor. This is someone who's been doing it for a while and can help you through the process.

A *mentor* usually comes at some price. A good one, someone who's doing this on a full-time basis themselves and has a proven track record, can charge you money. Or, if you can provide them some type of value outside money, that might be something too. For example, maybe you can trade them some sweat equity in exchange for mentorship, which would be a win-win.

Once you immerse yourself within the community, you shouldn't have any trouble with finding a mentor, as long as your level of commitment is there—to take us back to an earlier point.

Document all these individuals you're researching so you can organize who everyone is, which ones you need to get to know better, and which ones you need to stay away from. Believe it or not, there are pariahs in every industry—those are people that have developed a bad reputation.

We won't chase that rabbit too far, but I will say who you associate yourself with is a fundamental component of your overall strategy.

A good CRM system will help you build the right community to will move you toward your goals. There are a few good CRM systems out there, like Hubspot or Zoho, for example.

Furthermore, you'll want to know if you have the right tools to evaluate opportunities promptly from the community that you're building. Once you develop these *buying parameters*, you must stick to them. For example, I only invest in assets that I can control or have influence over and that produce cashflow. Now, I have numerous parameters beyond these, depending on the opportunity I'm vetting.

I've held myself close to those standards over the years, and it has served me well. This will lead you to the right assets, or they'll come to you as people in the industry start to recognize your parameters and reach out.

In terms of portfolio management (which we've only scratched the surface of) or if you're starting a business, client management starts with goal setting.

What is your action plan for managing these assets and clients after you start a business? This is very different from the win-win model of goal setting discussed earlier. That's more of an attainment cycle, while this is more about what you've already procured. You'll want a good project management system, or even just Quickbooks. I've been using Quickbooks to help me manage my portfolio for years.

If you work closely with a group of people, you can use those tools to share videos and create channels within the online forum to separate and organize conversations within different sectors of the business. It keeps everything in a very organized and collaborative state, and I can't recommend them enough.

It's important to look at what systems you have, both physically and digitally. Look at each one and see how they work off each other. In my case, I manage my portfolio of notes physically and digitally with cloud-based tools. I have systems that feed off each other. In certain cases, when I'm dealing with the portfolio management side, I don't like to look up information in a computer system in the cloud-based system, so I use physical paper and files for borrowers to look up their info, and that's just something that works for me. Now, many people I work with simply rely on the digital. They don't like *anything* that uses paper or folders—and in this day and age, I understand that. I guess I'm old school.

Now, the same way you instituted time management, you'll also have a work schedule mapped out for the management of those assets. This is important because any stream of income that's poorly managed risks ceasing to be a good stream of income for a variety of reasons, depending on your industry.

I've just published my fifth book, and the act of writing it is a great example. I walk through the fundamentals. I outline and then execute it. I approach the writing of that book not as a hobby but as a job that must be performed. I don't have room for error.

Some people look at starting a small business or new investment as a hobby, and I cannot caution against that enough. Starting a new business needs to be looked at like life and death.

This is what I've seen with hundreds of people coming into the real estate investing space and exiting within the same year. They came in, driven by some type of renovation show featuring some young man with long hair and great abs swinging a hammer. They're projecting. Seeing themselves as these individuals on TV. Maybe they even read some books on real estate investing to seek out their fundamentals.

Yet most of those people fail when it comes to execution because they are emotionally driven. The books help to understand the fundamentals, but mastery comes from execution.

Now, perhaps you work another job and it seems hard to take on new opportunities. This isn't to say that you should give that up. I wouldn't suggest that at all. As stated in previous chapters, I'm trying to help you add new income streams, not take them away right now.

My hope is that you won't become a statistic. You won't come into these endeavors, dabble a bit, and leave unsuccessfully. This book is meant to be a roadmap to help you get there.

When I talk about treating this like life or death, I'm saying you need to have a full-time commitment to *this*, even if you still have a day job. Once again, that involves having a plan, acting on that plan, developing the fundamentals over time, and mapping out your processes and metrics based on what you're learning. The measurements are things that need to be evaluated on an ongoing basis to make sure your performance is where it needs to be.

Furthermore, as you execute, think about who's around you. Think about what type of influence they have over you. One thing you can do is make a list of the ten people who are most important to you and determine if they're a positive or negative influence. Are they helping you move forward or not?

The problem is, most people lack the discipline to achieve success in life or in their careers. Put some time into building your win-win plan—both in the acquisition of the streams of income and the management of those streams.

You can multiply your efforts to bring in new streams of income, and the more proficient you become in underwriting, the more scalable you become. It's funny how that works. For example, I vet one note the same way I vet a hundred notes. So, why not buy a hundred notes instead of one?

Case closed.

As I scale, as I take on new streams of income, as I grow in my mission, the people around me benefit as well—which is really the endgame for the CFE.

Kill the negative thoughts and limiting beliefs. They'll hit you hard when you're first building out your plan, but also when you least expect while working on your plan. Negativity comes in many forms. I fight it every single day.

Robert Kiyosaki talks about the little child in each of us. For example, the little boy in you will say, "You can't do this. You're not big enough. You're going to fail."

That small child wants you to think you're a loser, and it happens time and again, not just in the upfront phases. Now, the more you keep pushing at those daily tasks, the less those thoughts will affect you.

I tell you they stop altogether, but they do get easier to work out over time as you're mastering the fundamentals.

What fears do you have? How do your fears control you? How do you guard your mind? Are you able to focus throughout the day or are you easily distracted?

People today are getting bombarded with information. Worse, many people have lost their jobs due to the COVID-19 pandemic and are wondering if they're going to get them back. I've met several people who have lost their jobs but are using the pandemic as a golden opportunity to start something new. They've been holding back for years. They haven't had time. They have resources saved, and they're going to make a run at it.

So, as we progress out of this pandemic, I think we're going to see a whole host of new businesses and new sentiments toward independence—which is awesome, and I welcome that day.

Be cautious. You must be alert for external factors that will try to throw you off your game. The more you do, the more the winds will blow against you. However, the more you overcome, the more you will grow. Life hits you from all sides. You have options for how to react.

The stronger you are with the Five Cs (Cash, Concentration, Creation, Community, Control), the more equipped you'll be to handle unexpected circumstances. They become your identity and will help drive you.

How will you journal your progress? I use a daily planner to help me capture my story, and knowing the roads I've taken helps me build my future road maps. It also helps me understand the tasks involved in accomplishing my goals. Understanding those goals allows me to focus on workflow, with all those tasks organized. I have operations manuals, as well, but it all starts with journaling.

Don't be short-sighted either.

When I started note investing, I failed to take in strategic partners. Your action plan can be bold and involve a lot of people, even if they don't know they're going to be brought into the fray. The plan has to start somewhere.

Think big.

It doesn't have to just be mom and pop. Those are fine, but every industry comes with people and resources and activity. Strategic partners will help you take a small action plan and produce big results.

This was a major mistake in my life. Across the street from where I owned a few commercial properties, there was a whole block for sale. It had a 5,000-square-foot building with three separate building spaces on several acres of land that were all zoned commercially. The block had been vacant for about six months. In 2011, the commercial real estate market wasn't moving quickly.

I could have picked up this property for around $1 million—a steal. I had this vision because I would sit in one of my offices, stare at this block, and say, "I don't have the down payment. I can't buy it. What if I can't find the tenants to occupy the space?" Even with these doubts, I would still visualize owning it. I could actually see landscaping vehicles coming in and out, a vehicle washing station, a new shed, and numerous tenants operating from within the space.

I would run calculations on what that meant in terms of potential. They were asking $1.1 million, but a broker told me I could probably pick it up for about $950,000. Still, all I could think about was how I didn't have the money for the down payment.

Flash forward a few months later. Someone bought the block and did exactly what I'd imagined. They had a landscaping company move in, the washing station, the shed, the whole nine yards. They even had a few churches fill in the other spaces. It was unbelievable. Someone else was realizing my vision.

They executed where I did not, so it was just a dream, not a goal. If it had been a goal—with a clear action plan—the execution would have occurred. I would be the one running the whole operation. But I thought small, and it hurt me on that one. Every time I think small, I think about the block that got away.

Looking back, I realize I could have tapped on a few shoulders and gotten the money I needed for that down payment.

When my wife and I started our museum exhibition company, we set it up to sell directly to the federal government on the prime level. We had all these large outfits, with their 100,000 square foot facilities. Those guys snubbed their noses at us. We were writing proposals on the same requirements for the same jobs as they were, but they didn't understand how us "small-town nobodies" working out the basement of our home with outdated equipment and one employee could do what they did with their elaborate operation. They would make fun of us. You could see it time in and time out when we'd go on site surveys for new projects. We were a running joke to them.

However, once we got established, started winning proposals, and took over contracts that they used to have, only then did they start to respect us. Then they wanted to partner with us. We did partner with them on certain occasions, but it was on our terms.

When you become the prime in a federal contract, you're at the closest point to the golden goose—which is the most profitable position to be in.

CHAPTER 8

Sharing is Caring

There is no delight in owning anything unshared.
—Seneca

This is the fifth book I've written. I'm proud because I already have some books that can help people improve their lives. What's more, I feel a sense of accomplishment that I've been able to build freedom of time in my life that allowed me to spend it giving back. I can take my time, formulate all these thoughts, and lay them out in a book format.

In a sense, it's really a reflection of what freedom has bought me—and how I use that freedom.

A lot of people focus purely on the results of time freedom, and it usually looks glamorous. Picture someone driving an expensive sports car or hanging out on the beach.

I prefer to show the results in the form of a giveback, which brings me the most satisfaction in life. Plus, it's on my Win-Win Cycle, so it furthers the momentum of that cycle. I can go right back into goal setting, but I can do even loftier goals next time or contribute more to the larger society, which is my end goal.

Of course, financial freedom and security for my family all come with it. It's a completely gratifying package deal.

For my readers, I hope that sharing some strategies and putting together a road map for building additional streams of income will help you get to where you're going, as well. The more you know and share, the better our world gets. It's amazing how the mind works. It can continue to create once you dedicate your life to sharing.

One mistake some people make is thinking they're only good in one niche or their thoughts somehow tap out at some point, but creativity is infinite. The more you apply your mind to being creative, the more you grow. Best of all, it's endless.

In my first book, *Note Investing Made Easier*, I mentioned having a brand with three pillars:

1. I operate a private mortgage fund with my business partner that helps homeowners stay in their homes with payments they can afford.
2. I operate an income fund with my partner that delivers monthly passive income to accredited investors.
3. I'm a thought leader and author that helps people become CFEs.

I'm also on various platforms and podcasts, which goes back to how sharing and caring creates its own momentum.

My three pillars came about because I wanted to create a brand that was based on helping people create more passive income on their lives. The more I can help others, the more they'll reciprocate. The more exposure in the industry, the larger the deal flow too. The increase in opportunities leads to an increase in status—and so on and so forth. Everything starts feeding off each other, if modeled out properly and executed.

My brand has grown over the years. This is the fifth book, and I've sold thousands of copies of the previous ones. I have dozens of people who reach out to me on a weekly basis for various reasons. Plus, to give you a sense of what my companies do in terms of volume, we've purchased over $40 million in mortgage debt in the past twelve months alone.

Why am I telling you this?

When you evolve your brand over time, and test and retest your model, you can start to measure your successes (or lack thereof) to other operations within your space. This helps me find opportunities to create additional partnerships, which allows for more win-win situations.

But imagine if I wasn't a magnet for deal flow. Imagine spending endless effort and energy, marketing and branding to the point of exhaustion. You're trying to find clients versus them finding you. That leaves this huge void of energy left for the opportunities on your plate.

The whole idea is to position yourself in such a way as to attract the deal flow to you. While we're imagining, doesn't that look so much better? It's way less frustrating. It should be looked at as an investment that may not pay off immediately but will pay off with time. That's how you build sustainability.

However, I think most individuals and small businesses spend their time chasing opportunities, which is very exhausting. Or they don't do it at all. How about that?

Also, if you build yourself as a magnet for opportunities, you'll be able to use that freed-up energy for scalability purposes.

I can tell you, there are numerous ways to benefit others. My wife can homeschool our four children, which is something that wouldn't have been possible several years ago. They will have a better shot, growing up, because they learned about how companies are run and entrepreneurship. We can also hire employees, like our children, who can make significantly more money than what we could have offered before.

If you set yourself upright, it's reciprocating.

We are serving more homeowners than ever as a compassionate lender who listens to them and works out terms they can afford. We are helping families with the best hedge against inflation (i.e., monthly passive income). And as we grow, we can give more back to charity, which is always important and warms the heart.

This is the win-win of it all in the end. The profit and additional streams of income are good, but it's really about the contribution and the effect you have on society. When you leave this planet, will society be in a better place? It should be, even if it's only a notch better.

Perhaps after reading this book, you'll flip the script and decide you now qualify to be a mentor or accountability partner to others. Many individuals have made that decision and created long-term streams of income as a result. People seeking opportunities, especially when they don't have their own sense of identity or clearly defined goals or focus, become susceptible to any number of people coming in and out of their lives. In the end, not everyone is a good partner and not every opportunity is a good one.

Also, if you're not driven by plans, with a clear sense of your goals and your brand, then you're driven by emotions. So, there aren't a lot of options. I'm not a psychologist, but there are only so many things that drive a person. When it's emotion, you're susceptible to all sorts of shady characters and situations.

That said, side with people who have goals, plans, and focuses that are in alignment with your values. At the same time, some people will look like a bandage to you. They might help propel you when you feel lost, when you don't know how to move forward, so you'll go for the shiny object. You'll go to the fool's gold.

It's not so much a knock on them (not always). You just don't always know right away if it's a good fit. You don't know if the longevity will be there with this person.

I always recommend, when connecting with people, treating it like you're dating. And there's something to be said for routine.

Yesterday, a protégé called me as I was writing and said, "Martin, we want to take your advice." Now, I had advised them to start a ladies' group within the note-investing industry. There weren't any, and it would be a good branding move. It's a male-dominated industry.

My protégé told me she wanted to get the group started and asked how to get it going.

The first thought that came to mind was routine. So, you first select the small group you want to start with. You need to build a schedule with an agenda. Maybe there will be calls every other week over which you cover points on the agenda. You will do video conferencing and set the routine. Now, that's the "dating" we speak of.

Set the date, then go on the date. From there start setting goals. What are the expectations of each member? It's not enough to say you're just going to meet up and chat about whatever's on your mind. If there's no structure, there's no focus. It would need to be a very serious and functioning thing to grow their businesses, so I explained that to my protégé. Every member, for example, needs to bring deal flow to the table if they are to retain membership in the group. Spell it out explicitly, so everyone will know what they need to adhere to. That way, everyone can benefit from group membership without anyone leeching without contributing. Bear in mind, deal flow is king, as it leads to streams of income regardless of the industry.

I'm very excited to see how far she takes it, and I know the group is in good hands. It's just like anything else in life: if you don't have goals and expectations, you have nothing to work for. There's no direction, no structure, and nothing can be accomplished in that manner.

I shared this story because my conversation with this protégé ties into what I'm doing with this book. You need to get out there and know as many people in your industry as you can. Observe them through a research process. If you see someone you think there could be some type of meaningful connection—through shared values or similar objectives or whatever—start a dating situation to try to progress it organically into a strategic partnership.

That's one of the things that connected my wife and me. My wife is gorgeous, and I love her to death, but I must admit that equal to her beauty and intelligence is the fact that we've gone through entrepreneurship together and have the same goals in life. She's been down every difficult, dark road by my side, as we've built ourselves up over the years.

Before releasing *Note Investing Made Easier* in 2017, I was a full-time note investor for five years, living a comfortable life with the results of my investments. I think it's important to pay your dues and spend your time executing your action plan, building your fundamentals, documenting as much as possible, and building your processes. Then, at a point where you feel like you can give back, start sharing as much as possible.

It doesn't happen without those processes, without those action plans, without those actions. It takes a lot of hard work, but believe me, you can get there too.

And keep in mind: sharing is caring!

CHAPTER 9

Doing for Others

If you create incredible value and information for others that can change their lives—and you always stay focused on that service—the financial success will follow.

—Brendon Burchard

I f I could impart any kind of message to you, it'd be to bet on yourself. Invest in yourself. Rely on yourself. And take back control for yourself!

That may mean getting uncomfortable with your current situation for a while so you might grow your WHY and begin doing for yourself. It will require taking control back of your life, your career, and your streams of income.

Thirty-nine million people are out of work as of the writing of this book, due to the pandemic. So many people are being controlled by external forces that it's sad. It's more imperative than ever to take back control of your financial situation so that you can do for yourself as well as those around you.

I'm reminded of the groundbreaking book, *Rich Dad, Poor Dad*. Robert Kiyosaki teaches us that people are in a rat race called life, where they have very little control over their circumstances.[8]

Why do we stay in this rat race for so long?

Earlier on, I noted that when I was younger, I was in the work-earn-money-spend-money-be-broke-again model. It wasn't until years later that I developed a win-win model and started doing for myself. I lacked the control I needed with school, which caused me great anxiety and my grades suffered.

Many other people are still running this same race, and they do so up until they retire or die, never having experienced the kind of true financial freedom—or freedom of time—they deserve. They repeat the cycle until they just can't work any longer.

Meanwhile, many people recognize—and talk about—how they need something more, not just from a financial perspective but from a satisfaction perspective. Yet they give more excuses for why it's not going to happen. They don't have partners who challenge them. Their significant others may not even be challenging them.

Focus on where you are now.

Does your spouse challenge you? Are you able to relay your hopes and dreams? Are the people around you committed to success beyond their present circumstances? Or are they holding you back? Who are the people closest to you? That's a reflection of how your future is going to look.

Mediocrity is accepted by society, while we often demonize those who actually achieve more. I was out with my family one day in Georgetown around the time Mitt Romney was running for president, and I saw someone taking pictures of a very expensive yacht. It was probably an $80-million-plus yacht, and it was docked in DC.

I approached him and said, "Now, that's a nice boat."

Although he was gawking at the boat himself, he said, "No one needs a boat like that! What a waste of money!"

He was spewing negativity to me about the boat, but at the same time, his actions showed me he was in awe. He snapped a few more pictures, and I can't recall everything he said, but it furthered my impression of outrage and awe.

I don't want to say people are confused. Rather, it feels like people want to be successful but don't always know how to make it happen or put in the work required to achieve it. Some people might suggest, "Do they really want it to begin with?"

Well, I'll leave that for the philosophers.

I do know, however, that at some point you must hit your **pain point**, where it hurts so bad and you're fed up so much that you say, "I'm going to dedicate all my time and resources to becoming consumed with bettering my financial situation!"

What's your pain point? (You could have more than one.) If you don't hit that point, you might do like some folks and drift into obscurity or even attempt to dabble with becoming a CFE as a hobby. I've seen many people with that attitude come into the real estate investing world, pay for expensive training, and end up not making it. Usually, in this case, the pain point is hit while exiting the opportunity.

Are you at your pain point yet? I ask because you should seek pain. If you don't know if you've hit that pain point that means you're ready to change your life, you should imagine it.

If you have to go away for the night or find some private time for reflection. Separate yourself from everyone. Visualize it. Then ask the following questions:

1. What can I remove from my schedule to make time to commit to putting my action plan together?
2. How can I manage my current schedule while setting aside blocks of time to devote to my action plan?
3. What changes do I need to make so that I prioritize maintaining a living financial statement?
4. What accountability partners do I need?
5. What are the financial goals that will allow me to meet my current expenses and live the life I want?

Visualize this new world, and what it might look like, and then compare it to your present state. Maybe there's a pain point to be had. I'm not a psychologist, but I can safely say you're going to want to seek out your pain point if you're not sure you've hit it.

Even though I'm fully committed to what I'm doing, I also feel pain points, so I know they're out there. I feel like I need to move the needle myself.

You should be welcoming that pain. It's just like people who work out at the gym. They seek to tear their muscles down so they can rebuild them. In other words, they seek out the pain because it stands in between them and where they're going.

Visualize how things should be. As you use Xmind to document your goals and create your action plan, keep in mind it doesn't always have to be in words. It may be in videos you make for yourself. Or you could do an audio recording that you play on repeat in your car so you can hear your own words and know where you're heading. There are numerous ways to reinforce your action plan in your mind. Whatever works best for you, as long as there's some type of daily affirmation of your goals.

When you build out your plan, the timeline needs to be cyclical. As you go around the Win-Win cycle (Goals, Activity, Fundamentals, Enhancing, Sharing) you build confidence, momentum, and mastery. You gain growth within each category of your plan. You become an even stronger goal-setter and achiever.

Those action plans make you stronger. You become more effective with your time management. You become more effective at journaling. You become more effective at building your operations manual and all the processes that go into that. You also get more effective at sharing, and as you do, you become a thought leader, and your brand increases.

So, you grow depth within each phase, and your plan will serve as your underlining strength as you build disciplines that get your financial house in order.

Treat the result of each phase of your action plan as a treat where you reward yourself.

My role as a promotions manager was one of the only things I took away from corporate America that I still use today. I believe you have to motivate people, starting with yourself. I had to motivate people in my call center, for example, to extend credit to customers. And when I found a good motivation, I laid it on thick.

As you achieve your goals, reward yourself. It may just be a dinner or a movie. You might knock off early on a workday or take the kids out to a park or someplace special. Whatever it is, you need to have some type of celebration.

Bring in mentors and action partners. As you grow your community, you need to seek people who are going to mean much more to you than a regular date. People you court intensely, looking to build a lifelong partnership through which you bring value to one another. That way it's done in a formal setting where expectations are set up front.

Sometimes it can come in the form of payment. If someone's very successful in an area you want to be successful in, why do they need to bring you up to speed? What's in it for them? You have to think from their perspective too. You might be creating an additional stream of income for them so they can help you create an additional stream of income for yourself, which is the best way to go. Or it could be in the form of bringing deal flow or opportunities to that individual in exchange for teaching you the ins and outs as you work those opportunities together.

What is a mentor? Washington University says, "A mentor may share with a protégé information about his or her own career path as well as provide guidance, educational support, and role modeling. A mentor may help with exploring careers, setting goals, making contacts, and identifying resources." Do you aspire to be one?

As you gain mentors in the industry, keep the end in mind. At some point, you will become a mentor to a protégé, which is extremely gratifying. You'll remember how your mentor was with you.

As you grow, think in terms of *accountability partners* too. An accountability partner is a person in the same industry or area who you can meet up with regularly to hold each other accountable on goals and aspirations. How do you find accountability partners and bring value to them?

We've touched on this before, but you can use https://meetup.com/, social media, or just go places that these potential partners would go (e.g., conferences). You could even call on some of the vendors that support the industry and get some feedback on how to find good potential partners.

No one is hiding on this planet anymore. Based on social media and the internet, the world has never been closer and more accessible than they are today, so get out there and make some connections.

Just keep in mind the goal: being able to give back at higher levels. That's your endgame, and you can do that through mentorships, having accountability partners, creating those action plans, performing those daily rituals, working on your personal brand and marketing, and fine-tuning your mastery through execution over time. These are the main ingredients for living a CFE life.

We talked a lot earlier about the Five Cs, and I'd be remiss to not adequately address Caring, as well, before concluding. The more control- and value-driven your life is, the more you can give back. Think of times you've given the most back, whether it was with your time or money. They were probably times when you were in the most control of your life and things were happening for you.

Think about it. People aren't inclined to give back when their lives are in chaos or they're having a lot of difficulties. They tend to be more guarded and secluded. Yet caring is the ultimate reward and marks a point of complete control under the CFE lifestyle.

We've all seen the advertisements online. Someone's marketing how to make a quick buck or build so-called passive income. They're sitting on a beautiful beach or driving a fancy car. We've all seen these images play out over and over again online and in traditional media. We may sometimes demonize people who are successful, but if most people are honest with themselves, they want to be successful too.

Nobody ever says, "I want to be a failure when I grow up." They simply have big dreams and aspirations that slowly fall by the wayside as they get older, more complacent, and more reliant on external factors. They completely relinquish control.

The sad reality is, when this occurs—this lack of self-control—not only are we harming ourselves but we're harming those we care about the most. We aren't able to care for others when we lack control over our own lives.

Being able to care at the highest level is at the heart of this book.

Most people have a caring heart, but the means to deliver the care are lacking, whether that's emotionally, mentally, spiritually, financially, or some combination of all four.

This book is not just about maximizing the caring but growing your care circle too; that is, growing your inner circle and caring for even more people.

Now, that's a WHY!

This occurs the more you utilize the Win-Win Cycle. You can be in a better position to care about more people, who, in turn, can also care about more people—and the cycle continues.

It's like I said from the onset: People see you by your actions, so make your actions awesome by building your house of discipline on multiple streams of income!

CHAPTER 10

How to Create Multiple Income Streams

Your problem is to bridge the gap which exists between where you are now and the goal you intend to reach.
—Earl Nightingale

I recently had the pleasure of discussing some ideas for this book with my friend and colleague, Chaim Ekstein. I value and cherish the relationship we've built together over the years, as well as his cooperation for this project and other projects we've collaborated on. Chaim is a certified financial planner, and he has helped numerous senior citizens and others create multiple streams of income over the years.

When we sat down for this book, in typical Chaim fashion, he shared several nuggets that I'd like to pass along to you— particularly all the different ways to create multiple streams of income in today's society.

Martin: In all your years of financial planning, what are some of the most effective ways you've seen people create multiple streams of income?

Chaim: Let's start with the areas where I don't see people generating income, and I think they should. There are treasure troves of opportunities out there for people, and it's a shame that more people don't take advantage. It bothers me when I see that because it's available to them. Martin, if you think about it, what is the biggest value a person has in their life or business?

Martin: I would have to say their knowledge.

Chaim: Their knowledge. That's true, but I think one of the biggest values they have—or could have—is their connections. Now, for example, you and I are talking about this because we know one another. One of the assets I have is my relationship with you. One of the assets you have is your relationship with me. And the same goes for all your contacts, friends, and associates.

Building all these relationships is one of the toughest challenges we face in business. I see this specifically with a lot of the seniors I work with. I'm working with people who have been in business twenty, thirty, forty years or more.

And when I talk business, it doesn't even have to mean your own business. It can mean your employment. Wherever you go and whomever you speak with, you're building up this tremendous asset, which is called your contacts or relationships. I call this *human capital*.

Once you have the connections, you can leverage them by providing different services. You can provide a different value. It doesn't have to be narrowed down to a specific offering that you do in your business. Unfortunately, most people don't take advantage of this innate ability to leverage their contacts.

You see this play out a lot on social media when one platform buys out another platform. The reason they do so may not even be about making money; they're buying them because they have a lot of contacts. They have a lot of people that use the platform.

But when people start talking about multiple streams of income, I see a lot of excuses being played out in their minds. For example, they might say, "No, I'm different. I can't because of this or that." But that's not true.

In terms of your readers, Martin, if they work at all in their life—and if they've been an honest person and trust themselves and have built relationships over time—they inherently already have what it takes. They can develop different streams of income, and much of the hard work is already done. They have a certain number of connections built-up already. I think that's a good foundation for this conversation. Would you agree?

Martin: I absolutely agree. This is something that's cultivated over time. It goes beyond merely making a few contacts on LinkedIn or Facebook. There's this whole long, drawn-out process of getting to know people.

Chaim: That's right. You have people online who may contact you and say hello or ask you for coffee, but I'm not really referring to those types of people. I'm talking about people you build trust with over time.

Once we establish that relationships are our most valuable commodity, the next part is how to build multiple streams of income. The typical way people do that is by passive income investments, real state, stocks that pay dividends, and so on. To create these additional streams, you typically need money. And if you have money, those can be great opportunities that people can look into. This is what most people are familiar with. Unfortunately, a lot of people don't have enough money to be involved in things like that.

Martin: If I'm understanding you correctly, the initial focus is on what resources you have—whether it's human capital or knowledge about a particular subject—as well as how you can leverage those things to create streams of income for yourself, which is different from deploying money to earn passive income.

Chaim: People's antennae should be on high alert when it comes to creating multiple streams of income, so it doesn't have to be one or the other. It can be both. The idea is that you can take whatever is available, not just a dichotomy between one thing and something else. You should be thinking, "What are the opportunities in front of me?" Often times, it's right in front of you, and you don't see it.

Martin: With human capital and leveraging whatever resources are at your disposal in mind, you can go into a particular area such as stock dividends. How does that work?

Chaim: Let's say you like AT&T. I'm not saying they're good or bad. I'm just giving you an example. So, AT&T is making a profit every year, and they have to split that profit up among the shareholders. If you buy shares in AT&T, you're a shareholder, so you're going to get a dividend. A lot of people know about stock investing in terms of having this asset appreciate in value. But very few people have a stock portfolio just for the purpose of stock dividends. This is a passive income stream. And when you start looking in this direction, you're not following the market as much. I don't care if the stock goes up or down as long as I'm getting my dividend every quarter, for example. You're probably not going to show up at an AT&T board meeting and tell them what their next moves should be. You trust their board. You trust that they'll make the right moves, and you sit back and collect your dividends. So, this is a very passive way of earning money.

Martin: When it comes to something like that—where you're only buying one share of a stock, for example, and you're earning a few bucks per quarter—it still serves as an additional stream of income, which lends to a particular proof of concept. You need to be doing that, but maybe on a larger level?

Chaim: Yes, and of course, we're talking about AT&T. But let's say down the block from where you live, there's a business, and you know the owner. You know they could use some extra capital to expand, and you make a partnership or strategic alliance with them to earn some profits that way. This is another area where you can get some passive income going without doing anything.

You know, Martin, a while back I was talking to a friend who went into an interesting line of business. He started buying a product in bulk at a very good price before reselling for a profit. Now, most of the time, when he took the purchase order, he already had a buyer. So, it was already sold.

For example, let's say he bought product x at $100,000 in bulk and sold it for $120,000. That's a profit of $20,000. As I noted, when he bought the product, he usually had a customer, but he had to pay upfront, COD. He collected the money thirty days after delivery, so that meant he had $100,000 sitting there for about a month—money he couldn't use. That's the only way to make that work. He had to pay the upfront money, and he couldn't get paid for about thirty days. And he made $20,000 profit after that. It put a big stress on his business, and he couldn't grow like he wanted to because his capital was always tied up.

One day, I asked him to imagine what it would mean if he had an extra $100,000 in capital for his business at any given moment. He said it would have a tremendously positive effect. But he already had all the credit he could get, so I made a partnership with him.

"The next time you have another deal and can use $100,000," I told him, "come to me. I'll give you the $100,000, and we'll split the profit." It'll be 10 and 10. That's $10,000 each. He's happy because he wouldn't have made the deal without the capital. I was happy because I made a beautiful return of 10% in one month. It was another stream of income.

To take us back to our original point, for me to make the deal, I had to know the guy. I had to understand his business, and he had to know me. It was only for those reasons that I was able to leverage our relationship and earn an additional stream of income.

It's food for thought. We can be talking about any number of different relationships, but the same general rules should apply. The whole point is to make people stop and think about the treasures they already have in their back pockets. Your readers should be thinking about how to create win-win situations for themselves and others.

Martin: That's a wonderful point. For there to be an opportunity, it starts with that person or contact. There's no *realized return* without that connection.

Chaim: Correct. It starts at the point of connection. It then goes into the conversations, then the curiosity, then the brain. Let me explain. If you approach your friends and relationships passively, deals may never come about. Instead, you should be developing a curiosity about how to leverage your relationships to create deal flow.

For instance, you could ask a friend what their business struggles are. Or you could ask them if there are any opportunities that you both can take advantage of. If you start making it your business to understand what's going on with friends and connections, good things can come about. Now, obviously, that's not always going to be the case, but you'll increase your chances.

Martin: Turning to real estate, you and I are both landlords. We both own commercial and residential properties. Let's say there's a rental property that you're going to pay $100,000 for. Closing costs come to $1,000, and remodeling costs come to $8,000. Your total investment in this opportunity is $109,000. You then rent this property out, and from that point, you receive $1,200 in rent per month. After the first twelve-month period, you've earned $14,400 in rental income. In terms of expenses, you have taxes, utilities, and insurance, and let's say that comes out to $3,000 annually. You'll minus those expenses from your gross revenue to get an annual return of $11,400.

To calculate the return on investment for that type of opportunity, you'll divide the annual return of $11,400 into the total investment of $109,000, which yields an ROI of 10.4% per year, and that's good positive cashflow. Do you have any thoughts on this *buy-and-hold real estate strategy*?

Chaim: I think it makes sense in some situations. 10.4% return on your money. You invest $109,000 upfront, and you're left with a net positive income of $11,400 per year, I think it's beautiful. You'll agree that you must account for the condition and quality of the house. Eventually, you're going to have to put in more money. You have to account for the type of tenants you're going to take. Are you looking for people with good income and good credit? Or are you going to run the risk of having to evict people and things like that? Not to mention, this 10.4% return is without taking any leverage—without taking any mortgage. If you take a mortgage at today's interest rate of 3–4%, that 10.4% return could become 14–16%.

Now, your investment is looking even better, but the point is, people should know it's doable. You just have to make it your business—and make it happen. Unfortunately, many people are very passive about these concepts. They think they don't really know much about real estate, for example. But that's just because they haven't become curious enough about it to become knowledgeable. That's why I said you have to make it your business to know, and then you will know!

Martin: Let's explore the notion of leverage further for my readers. So, originally, we said our real estate investor had $100,000 upfront for a specific opportunity. Now, imagine you take some leverage by way of a mortgage. But you can put $20,000 down on that same property and take out a mortgage for $80,000. You can do this five times and buy five similar properties for that same $100,000, versus buying and holding one property with no leverage and earning 10%.

Chaim: Exactly. Of course, whenever you calculate a cashflow rate of return on any real estate opportunity, you also have to consider that the property value may go up—or *appreciate*—over time. For example, the neighborhood is getting better, there's less inventory, supply and demand, inflation, and so on. Whatever the case, you must also consider that your asset may be appreciating whether you take any leverage or not. But as long as you have a good, healthy cashflow and the opportunity to appreciate, why not?

Martin: Another area I've looked at but never put any real energy or effort into is *product licensing*. The author Harvey Reese has a book called *How to License Your Million Dollar Idea*. He gives readers a whole game plan with which they can think of an idea that can be offered to a company so they can create a product around it and pay them royalties. So, you think of an idea, build a prototype, and market it to businesses that can then turn your product into something tangible to sell. Reese also partners with people, sometimes. If he likes their idea, they enter a 50/50 partnership in terms of producing and placing the product and earning royalties.

Here's an example, to bring this to life. My sister is a horse trainer. Part of the process of warming up a horse involves what's called lunging, where you run them in a circle. You have to use a lunge whip to move them in the direction you want them to go. Whenever she uses the whip, she has to make a light clicking sound with her tongue. So, one day, she got the idea to attach an automatic clicker to the lunge whip, so she wouldn't have to make that sound manually.

Soon afterward, she went to work and created a prototype. I later helped her introduce the idea to a few horse-supply companies, and one of them contracted with us. They gave us a down payment to start producing and distributing the product. We made a little bit of money, but it was something that eventually died out. Have you ever gone down the road into intellectual property?

Chaim: I developed a patent once, but I never did anything with it. It was over twenty years ago. A lot of people are afraid of the unknown. If my grandparents had had that opportunity, I would understand. But nowadays with Google and the internet, there's so much information available to us, so there's no excuse. Of course, I'm talking to myself too. It's like the patent. I didn't take it to the next level, but maybe if I read that book I will.

It is interesting, though, that you bring this up because people have a lot of ideas, but they're too humble. "Who am I to bring a product to the marketplace?" You don't need to know too much. You just need to know that there are people who *do* understand how to do these things, and those people are waiting for you to contact them. They're willing and able to help you make it happen.

Martin: Thank you, Chaim. Now, government contracting is another area in which I have multiple streams of income. As you know, my wife and I started a company that sold to the federal government on the prime level. The federal government is the largest buyer of goods and services in the world, per numerous sources. There's $1 billion in new opportunities posted every day in terms of contracts and solicitations.

They sign over eleven million contracts per year. About 95% of the contracts are awarded to small- and medium-sized businesses like my company, which is still operating. However, less than 5% of US businesses work with the federal government. They have tons of programs for lending and designations, which you can receive whether you're a minority, woman, or veteran-owned business, for example.

The point is, there are millions of opportunities out there for new businesses to set themselves up and sell to the largest buyer in the world. Anyone interested in some of the areas available can visit https://beta.SAM.gov/ and begin their research there. You can also register to sell to the federal government at https://SAM.gov/.

I wrote the book *Secrets to Winning Government Contracts*, so I get some royalties from it every month, as well as through prime contracts that my company still holds.

Chaim: I love this subject, and I'd like to jump in on that one, Martin. You know, maybe it's just part of your DNA and who you are as a person, but let's think about it through the lens of your readers.

They should be sitting back and just looking at what's in front of their eyes. Here's a person who started in a certain area, then began adding businesses and opportunities throughout his life. Best of all, as he added these opportunities and increased his own skillset and knowledge, he made the world aware of what he was doing and giving back. You have books, workshops, mentorship programs, and more. And if you think about the value the world is receiving from a person like Martin Saenz, who's not holding that value inside but bringing it to life, it's quite simply tremendous.

If you think about what Martin is getting out of it, there are royalties and other streams of income that have slowly manifested over the years. In other words, for every bit of value he's putting out, he's receiving value for himself in the process, which is truly a win-win.

If you're looking for a role model, look no further. Don't be Martin Saenz or Chaim Ekstein, be yourself. But use people like Martin as role models and mentors. Think about what your experiences are, think about your connections, and become more curious about how to leverage those things because those are all assets.

The problem is, when most people obtain some skill, they bottle it all up on the inside. They think, "Hey, it's simple. It's no big deal." Well, of course, it's simple for them. But it's not so simple for the person looking to acquire that same skill or bit of information. The average guy needs someone with experience to show him how you did it.

So, my biggest takeaway from all this is, if you want proof that you can build multiple streams of income, look no further than the author. Once you do that, you'll know you can do it— and the book just becomes more of a "how-to" make it happen.

Martin: Thank you, Chaim. That's very humbling. And it'll segway nicely into my next point as well. Let's talk about publishing. You're an author. You've written a successful book. Writing a book and offering it up on Amazon is another source of potential income.

I'd just tell my readers, if that's something they're interested in, to start with an outline. *From that outline, start writing a rough draft, whether you have to break that up into small chunks each day over the course of several months or you squeeze it into a tighter window. Just make sure to have an editor clean it up.*

Have an image designed for the book cover. Create internal images for the book. You can find all these different freelancers on Fiverr who can help you with that. Have the editor who helps you clean up the content also help you put it on Amazon. For anyone who hasn't done that, it can be pretty tricky, at least the first go around.

Once they do that it'll be on the Amazon KDP platform to be sold. You can get started at https://kdp.amazon.com/. Plus, you can even have a voiceover person do an Audible version for you. Nowadays, a lot of consumers prefer to have an audio version of their book instead a physical or digital copy because they can fit it into their schedule better, perhaps as they're driving or on their phones. Since you've successfully written an awesome book, yourself, what suggestions would you give my readers?

Chaim: First, most people who've never written a book think it's like traversing Mount Everest. But everything is tough until you do it. It's like the little baby who first starts walking. It's tough for them at first, but everything is tough until you start doing it. From there you figure out how to do it, and the rest is pretty easy.

Writing a book is no different. I'd even say—before starting an outline—the first thing you need to do is to make a decision. You need to decide you're going to write a book. You can decide you're going to write a book about a certain subject, or you can just decide you're going to write a book and then figure out the *what*, taking us back to the point of ideation. If you decided you're going to write a book, then you're going to be successful because you're going to figure out how to do it.

Moreover, people can get stuck on pretty much anything. If something doesn't work right the first way, make sure you keep trying. Trust the decision that you made. Believe me, if you never decide to write a book, you're never going to write a book. Number one is to make a decision. Agreed?

Martin: One hundred percent. And once you do it, you've created revenue streams. Each book creates royalty checks each month, and I've created online courses to complement those books as well. To do that, I drafted a slide deck in PowerPoint. I had it edited. I had it redesigned by freelancers on Fiverr. I recorded the video sessions myself using Zoom, then uploaded those videos to Teachable and offered them on my website. There wasn't a lot of cost upfront, other than the fees I pay Teachable and the design work.[9]

The important thing is, if you have a laptop and a voice, you can create multiple streams of income using what you already know, whether that's through an e-book, paperback book, Audible, online course, or another offering. The idea is to create a stream of income by sharing your knowledge about a particular subject.

Chaim: Thank you for sharing that, and I agree, it's very straightforward. Teachable has made a beautifully simple-to-use product. It's easy, and everyone can do it.

If you think about it, now you're writing these books and more people are going to be associated with you, so the human capital increases. You have a platform like this book to educate people, but they also learn about your other products. And when they use those other products, they can learn about other investment opportunities. One thing is leading to the other, and it's wonderful. Everything starts working together for the greater good. So, in other words, step 5 isn't as hard as the first one.

Here's the best analogy I can give your readers: let's say you're climbing up a building that has twenty floors, but the elevator starts on the seventh one. Those first seven floors are going to be pretty tough, but once you get to that point, the remaining floors go much smoother and faster.

Martin: There's a snowball effect as your confidence and knowledge grow. You're technically getting better too, but it all comes with commitment. Commitment is not something you do.

Commitment is doing *x, y, z* on an ongoing basis, like a ritual—which is precisely what we discuss in the new book.

Chaim: I remember when I started my first book. My schedule was too busy for me to get it done, so I started getting up an hour earlier every morning. The first week was tough, and I felt tired all the time. But by the second week, I was used to it. The ball was rolling—and it was picking up speed.

Martin: Let's say you have an online course now, and you're providing value to readers all over the world. You can also do live courses. There's a need for social interaction and people to meet in person. Some people learn better that way. We're deeply social creatures, so you can offer live courses as an additional stream of income too. As noted throughout the book, this idea was COVID-inspired, and live courses are particularly big right now while more people are spending time at home.

Chaim: You just have to be flexible and see what the needs are and what the timing is like in your life. If you don't adapt to change, what may have once been profitable could become a burden. For example, in ten years, maybe online courses aren't as popular as they were, but you'll be fine as long as you can sense the change and adapt.

Martin: Well, hopefully, those courses stay popular a little bit longer—but you're absolutely right. You have to be flexible when vetting new opportunities because things inevitably change.

In terms of the online courses, though, putting those together is pretty straightforward. We discussed creating a slide deck on PowerPoint, outlining it, creating a rough draft, having it edited by a professional, then having some designs created by a designer on the Fiverr platform. Once you have your course created you can place that on Teachable, your own website, or Udemy.

You know, we haven't discussed this explicitly, but we're also talking about using freelancers, which is fundamentally about putting ideas together by utilizing other people's strengths.

Let's say you're interested in doing a course on something you're knowledgeable about, but you're not the best editor. That's why I say you can find them on Fiverr, as well as designers or other freelancers as needed. These are people who do not perform the function of full-time employees, so the cost is lower. If you had enough hours in the day—and abilities in enough areas—you might not need outside contractors, but sometimes they're necessary.

It's just like sitting around a hotel room and getting hungry. You can connect with a DoorDash or GrubHub delivery person on an app and have fresh food delivered to your door. So, the days when we needed a whole in-house staff to get a lot of our tasks done are no more. We can get a lot of these tasks done online with ease—and typically for much cheaper than having full-time employees.

Chaim: Yes, everything is getting much simpler than it used to be. But let me ask you, do you also work with people in person?

Martin: Yes, I also have live workshops that are conducted in small groups of up to ten people. They make for a great getaway, but they're also all-inclusive regarding what you'll need to successfully launch and manage your note business.

Chaim: That's wonderful. You and I have worked together a lot, and I've noticed that you've also taken on a lot of protégés, correct?

Martin: From all this training comes the need for some individuals to have a more hands-on mentor to guide them. I work tirelessly with these protégés to get them where they need to be in community-building, branding, and identity. They can latch onto me, learn things I know, and expedite their growth. It lessens their learning curve.

Chaim: Do they have to pay an upfront fee to do that?

Martin: Absolutely. You have to pay one way or the other, whether it's through the tough lessons learned or through mentorship. Many people go with the latter and enter my mentorship program. Because my time is so limited, I have to be very selective. If any of my readers or listeners are interested, they can go to my site and find more information on that opportunity, as well.

Chaim: Hey, that's fantastic. Having seen you in action, I can say that anyone who gets into that program is very fortunate. The day you call them and tell them they're getting in is a very good day indeed.

Martin: I appreciate that, Chaim. But I must say, the intention of this book is to give people ideas of where they can start creating additional streams of income. It's so they can take back control of their lives. And it's so they don't have to be reliant on that one employer for income.

In many cases, a person's employer is holding them back from being the best they can be. So, this is very much a book about freedom—of both time and money. To get to where you have that kind of freedom, you have to take back control over your life!

Chaim: That's what I like about you, Martin. Your model has always been about developing win-win scenarios for everyone involved.

At this point, in closing, I'd like to tell your readers a brief story about an old client of mine who was in the kitchen-remodel business. He was good at developing trust with anyone he worked with, and he would come into the houses of people who were in the middle of renovations. Now, most of the time, when a person is doing a renovation, a For Sale sign is about to hit the front lawn.

He eventually realized that if a house could be staged before being sold, the value would go up a lot. He was very creative, and he reached out to and made a strategic alliance with a staging company. Plus, he mentioned to the homeowners that when they finished renovating, they should reach out to the staging company too. The center point of this business model was his relationships and the trust he built with multiple people.

He went from selling new kitchens to people to making a deeper connection with them and introducing the staging person into the equation. It was a win-win-win situation. No, in fact, it was win-win-win-win all the way around.

This helped the buyer get a better look at the house and envision its truest potential. When properly staged, a home will come alive. It helped him earn more money. It helped his new partner, the stager, earn more money. And it helped the property owners earn more money at closing.

Martin: Thank you for sharing that. You are correct. When everyone wins, it's a healthier, more sustainable model. That's excellent! Thank you for joining us, Chaim.

ENDNOTES

[1]https://www.broadbandsearch.net/blog/average-daily-time-on-social-media

[2]https://www.chamberofcommerce.org/

[3]https://www.statista.com/statistics/200838/median-household-income-in-the-united-states/

[4]https://www.pbs.org/newshour/economy/making-sense/3-charts-that-explain-the-rise-in-u-s-household-income

[5]https://www.vocabulary.com/dictionary/control?family=Control

[6]https://www.huffpost.com/entry/the-power-of-writing-down_b_12002348

[7]https://www.goodreads.com/quotes/tag/procrastination

[8]https://www.amazon.com/Rich-Dad-Poor-Teach-Middle/dp/1612680194

[9]https://www.teachable.com/

Made in the USA
Middletown, DE
23 August 2024